Lord of the Flies

William Golding

A GCSE revision guide
devised and written by Janet Oliver

The right of Janet Oliver to be identified as Author of this Work has been asserted by her in accordance with the Copyright, Designs and Patents Act 1988

Excerpts from Lord of the Flies by William Golding reproduced by kind permission of Faber and Faber Ltd.

First published 2020

ISBN 978-1-9163827-1-8

© Vega Publishing LTD 2020

Vega Publishing LTD, 12 Glebe Avenue, Woodford Green, Essex
IG8 9HB United Kingdom

Design by Martin Cadwallader

Contents

Introduction
How to use this book

'Lord of the Flies' is one of William Golding's most famous novels. The story of the stranded schoolboys' descent into evil is a compelling one which raises plenty of interesting questions about what happens to humankind when the constraints of civilised society are removed. Its universal appeal is obvious but tackling such a wide-ranging novel in a short exam is a real challenge.

This guide is written and laid out to help you with your revision of 'Lord of the Flies' and to ensure that your examination response is focused and clear. It is designed to show you how to include all of the key elements that the examiner is looking for:

- language analysis
- effective use of quotations
- exploration of themes
- understanding of character
- the contextual influences at the time Golding was writing

The book is divided into sections of characters and themes with a box at the top of each section which gives a strong, clear overview of the character or theme.

The section is then dealt with using 5-8 key quotations.

The analysis of each quotation relates directly to the theme or character. Some of the points are fairly straightforward and some are much more analytical. Quotes in the text are in **bold** font. Literary devices are in ***bold italics***.

The context is added at the end to show how it can be woven into an answer with a relevant quotation. Context means the social, historical and literary influences of the time that Golding was writing in and how these are reflected in the novel.

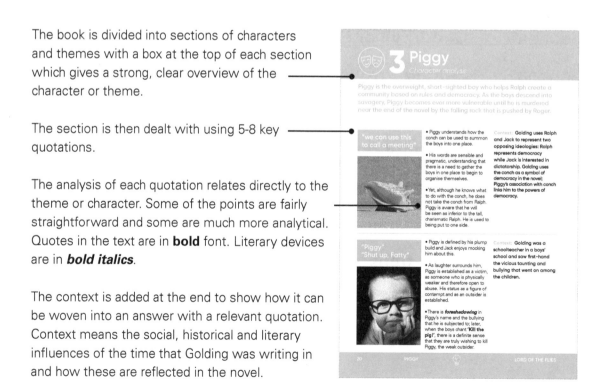

There is also a yellow box entitled 'Grade 9 Exploration' in each chapter. This shows you how you can look at alternative interpretations of the novel, which are crucial for gaining a grade of 7 or above.

Look out for the colourful mindmap. It condenses four main points from the chapter, including the Grade 9 Exploration box, into four strands.

The information is in a shortened format; if you want to keep your revision really focused, use the mind map to make sure you remember the key features of the chapter.

Next comes a sample essay question. This is based on an extract from the text and the question is underneath. Depending on which exam board you are using, the wording will be different but that's fine; the essay question and plan will still be incredibly useful.

The sample essay answer follows. This is based on a 4-5 paragraph formula which answers the question clearly and analytically. The font is small as there is so much detail but, if you are wondering what a top level answer looks like, do read it carefully.

Below that there is a box with essential exam tips: lots of good ideas and reminders that will help you on exam day.

At the back of the book, you will find a handy glossary of all the literary terms with examples and there's a list of the quotations, complete with chapter references.

Timeline
Plot Summary

The plot of 'Lord of the Flies' follows the adventures of a group of schoolboys who are stranded without adult supervision on a deserted island. It is unclear how long the boys are on the island for; what is clear is that the boys soon begin to descend into evil and those who try to cling onto civilisation are hunted to the death.

Chapter 1 – **The Sound of the Shell**

The novel opens with the boys realising that they are stranded on a deserted island without any grown-ups. Ralph and Piggy meet first and use the conch to call a meeting. Once all the boys are together, they elect a leader: Ralph. Ralph, Jack and Simon explore the island.

Chapter 2 – **Fire on the Mountain**

At a meeting, the boys begin to organise themselves. A littlun first mentions the beast but is laughed at. The boys collect wood for a fire to attract rescue. The fire burns out of control and kills one of the smaller boys.

Chapter 3 – **Huts on the Beach**

Tension is sparked as Jack starts to hunt and Ralph wants to build shelters. Simon withdraws into the woods by himself for quiet contemplation.

Chapter 4 – **Painted Faces and Long Hair**

Roger throws stones at the littluns, only just aiming to miss. Jack paints his face to help with his hunting. A ship is sighted but the fire has gone out and so their chance at rescue is lost. Jack returns from his first successful hunt and there is an argument about the hunters letting the fire go out. As they eat the roasted meat, tensions simmer and Ralph calls a meeting.

Chapter 5 – **Beast from Water**

Ralph tries to use the meeting to remind the other boys about the everyday needs of the community and the importance of being rescued. The beast is mentioned again and this time there is less laughter and more fear. Simon's attempt to explain that the beast is within them is not understood. Tensions rise again and Jack leaves the meeting with his hunters.

Chapter 6 – **Beast from Air**

Eric and Sam are on fire duty when they see the dead corpse of the pilot, still attached to his parachute. Convinced it is the beast, they run back to warn the other boys. The bigger boys head off in search of the beast. On their way, they discover Castle Rock.

Chapter 7 - **Shadows and Tall Trees**

While resting, Ralph daydreams about his home in Devon. Later, the boys catch a pig and, while acting out their triumph, begin to hurt one of the boys. Jack and Ralph, by now in almost continual conflict, climb the mountain and see the parachutist. Believing it to be the beast, they run away.

Chapter 8 - **Gift for the Darkness**

The boys hold another meeting where Jack challenges Ralph's position as chief. When no one supports him, he leaves the group. Ralph and Piggy light the rescue fire and realise that other boys have left the community to join Jack. Jack's new group of hunters kill a pig and leave the head on a stick as an offering for the beast. Jack and some of his tribe steal burning branches from Ralph's fire and invite them to a feast. Simon talks to the Lord of the Flies, the pig's head, who warns him of the danger they are all in from themselves.

Chapter 9 - **A View to a Death**

Simon sees the dead parachutist for what it is and runs to tell the others that there is no beast to fear. They are in the middle of a feast with wild dancing and chanting which becomes ever more frenzied as a storm breaks. In the darkness, Simon breaks out into the group of boys. They hack him to death. His body floats out to sea.

Chapter 10 - **The Shell and the Glasses**

Most of the boys have joined Jack's tribe. The few who are left pretend not to know anything about Simon's murder. Jack and his hunters attack their camp and, after a short fight, make off with Piggy's glasses to light a fire.

Chapter 11 - **Castle Rock**

Ralph, Piggy, Sam and Eric head off to Jack's camp in Castle Rock to reclaim the glasses. Piggy carries the conch to try to remind the tribe of the importance of their earlier community values. There is a furious confrontation between Jack and Ralph. Sam and Eric are seized by force. Roger levers a heavy rock which falls down and knocks Piggy to his death on the rocks below, the conch smashing as he falls. Ralph runs away as the hunters throw spears at him.

Chapter 12 - **Cry of the Hunters**

When it is dark, Ralph sneaks close to Castle Rock to speak to Sam and Eric who are on sentry duty. They warn him that Jack and Roger are planning to hunt Ralph down and kill him. Ralph hides in a dense thicket. The next day, the hunt begins as Sam and Eric are tortured to reveal Ralph's hiding place. The hunters light a fire to flush Ralph out and, as the fire spreads out of control, Ralph is chased across the island. On the beach, he is saved from death by the arrival of a naval officer and his men who have seen the fire and come to rescue them.

Ralph is the protagonist of the novel. He is elected as chief of the group of boys and tries to keep the community functioning and safe. Yet he is unable to stop the community degenerating into savagery and, at the end, he is hunted almost to the death by the other boys.

'a mildness about his mouth and eyes that proclaimed no devil'

- Ralph is a character who has an innate goodness. The **noun** **'mildness'** suggests a genuine kindness of heart.

- Golding uses the **motif** of eyes throughout the novel to explore ideas; Ralph's eyes reflect his humanity, and sharply contrast to the later description of Jack's eyes which are very different as they are **'ready to turn to anger'**.

Context: It is possible to read 'Lord of the Flies' as a religious **allegory**; the story of Adam and Eve's fall from grace in the Garden of Eden. Golding describes Ralph with religious **imagery** - 'mild' 'no devil' - and this **foreshadows** his loss of innocence by the end of the novel.

'him with the shell'

- Ralph quickly becomes leader of the boys, winning the vote to decide on the chief.

- He is elected partly because of his association with the conch. The conch is used as a **symbol** of civilisation in the novel and Ralph becomes the democratically elected leader. He represents democracy in the novel.

Context: Freudian analysis suggests that Ralph represents the 'ego', the part of us that struggles to resist our basic instincts and to comply with society. Ralph's link with the conch reflects this.

'true leadership'

- Golding describes Ralph as having **'true leadership'**. He shows good instincts as a leader, making sensible decisions about shelters and latrines.

Context: Ralph represents civilised society and the paternalistic aspects of government, trying to make sure that the community stays healthy and safe.

| **'Ralph was fighting to get near, to get a handful of that brown, vulnerable flesh'** | • Ralph gets caught up in the taunting of Robert when the boys pretend that he is a pig and use him in a play-hunt which hovers on the edge of real violence.

• Ralph does have a **'devil'** in him after all; he is attracted to the violence. The **_repetitive clause_ 'to get'** captures his burning desire to hurt Robert. In the heat of the moment, Ralph does not see Robert as a frightened human; the **_noun_ 'flesh'** reflects how Ralph has dehumanised Robert in his craving to overpower and inflict pain on him. | **Context:** Golding fought in World War 2 and saw even the best of men give in to savagery and brutality. Ralph's desire to hurt and kill is part of our nature and what Golding saw as the 'terrible disease' of being human. |

| **'the rules are the only thing we've got!'**
 | • Ralph is aware of the importance of rules as the foundation of their society.

• Ralph has a rational brain; he is able to think logically and clearly about what their community needs, such as the need for fire.

• The **_exclamatory sentence_** captures his passion; Ralph knows that the existence of their fragile society hangs on a knife edge and he is desperate to keep the community functioning.

• Ralph clings to the remnants of society and civilisation as he remembers it. | **Context:** Golding uses Ralph and Jack to represent two schools of thought on how society should be run: Ralph represents democracy while Jack is moving towards a dictatorship. In this, Golding draws parallels with the recent World War 2, often viewed as a struggle between opposing ideologies. |

| **'We'll go and look'** | • Ralph shows bravery when he announces his intention of climbing the mountain to see if there is a beast.

• The **_declarative sentence_** and the **_modal verb_ 'will'** work together to show Ralph's clear sense of purpose. Even though he is frightened, Ralph still leads the boys up the mountains. | |

• At the end, Ralph is hunted by the other boys and bursts out of his hiding place **'screaming, snarling, bloody'**.

• Ralph is no more than a savage himself at the end. The *list* highlights this as he is inarticulately **'screaming'** and **'snarling'**. Language is one of the defining features of civilisation yet Ralph makes animal noises. Fear has reduced him to animal status as he is focused on no more than a will to survive.

Grade 9 Exploration:
Look at the character in a different way

Is Ralph the hero of the novel?

Yes: Ralph is the central figure in the novel and has heroic qualities with his desperate attempts to resist the descent into savagery. He even looks like a hero with **'his size, and attractive appearance'** and his authority is sealed with his finding of the conch. According to literary conventions, Ralph is the hero of 'Lord of the Flies'. We see most events through his eyes and the novel follows his story, starting and ending with his experiences so that in the last page **'Ralph wept for the end of innocence, the darkness of man's heart, and the fall through the air of the true, wise friend called Piggy'**. There is a huge *pathos* in Ralph's tears as he acknowledges how he has lost his childhood and witnessed unspeakable acts; the reader feels empathy with this central character and his desperate sadness.

In this sense, the novel is a *bildungsroman*, a genre where the central character or hero learns maturity. Ralph has learnt about the dark side of human nature and cannot forget this, returning to civilisation a changed character.

No: There are other contenders for the title of hero. There is Piggy, who is the one who actually understands how to use the conch and instructs Ralph, knowing that the sound will call the others. It is Piggy who has the real knowledge and intelligence. Simon is also a contender with his pure qualities and his tragic death. Furthermore, Ralph himself is not the noble hero we might expect; he is certainly involved in the dreadful murder of Simon, showing that he is as capable of savage violence as the others. Indeed, perhaps Golding presents a bleak world of human savagery where all suffer from the 'terrible disease' of being human, and in this world there are no heroes.

Essential Exam Tip

☑ Read the novel at least once on your own. Ideally, re-read it a final time in the weeks leading up the exam.

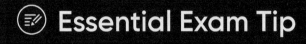

The conch is used as a *symbol* of civilisation in the novel and Ralph becomes the democratically elected leader. He represents democracy in the novel.

The *exclamatory sentence* captures his passion; Ralph knows that the existence of their fragile society hangs on a knife edge and he is desperate to keep the community functioning.

'him with the shell'

'the rules are the only thing we've got!'

Ralph is the elected leader.

Ralph tries to maintain civilisation on the island.

Ralph

Ralph is no more than a savage himself at the end.

Is Ralph the hero of the novel?

'screaming, snarling, bloody'

Yes: Ralph is the central figure in the novel and has heroic qualities with his desperate attempts to resist the descent into savagery.

Fear has reduced him to animal status as he is focused on no more than a will to survive.

No: Piggy and Simon are possible heroes. Alternatively, Golding presents a bleak world of human savagery where perhaps there can be no heroes.

Sample GCSE Exam Question

How far is Ralph the hero of the novel?

Sample GCSE Answer

☑ Introduction: give an overview of the idea of Ralph as a hero

A hero is usually the main character of a novel and one who the writer encourages the reader to admire. In 'Lord of the Flies', Golding appears to place Ralph neatly into this role of hero as he is swiftly elected as chief of the group of boys and tries to keep the community functioning and safe. Yet Ralph is certainly not flawless and there are other contenders for the title of the hero of 'Lord of the Flies'.

☑ Start with the point that Ralph is the protagonist of the novel

Golding establishes Ralph as the protagonist of the novel from the opening pages when the boy with fair hair clambers through the jungle. Golding uses Ralph's physical appearance to present a character who seems heroic with **'his size, and attractive appearance'**, and further physical details appear to reflect a character who has an innate goodness. Ralph has a **'mildness'** in his eyes that **'proclaimed no devil'**, the *noun* **'mildness'** suggesting a genuine kindness of heart. It is possible to read 'Lord of the Flies' as a religious *allegory* of the story of Adam and Eve's fall from grace in the Garden of Eden, and Golding describes Ralph at the start with religious *imagery*: 'mild' 'no devil'. This *foreshadows* his loss of innocence at the end of the novel as he, like Adam and Eve, acquires knowledge of evil. Golding uses the *motif* of eyes throughout the novel; the **'mildness'** of Ralph's eyes reflect his humanity, and sharply contrast to the later description of Jack's eyes which are very different as they are **'ready to turn to anger'**, suggesting how quick Jack will be to turn to violence. Golding uses Ralph and Jack to present ideas of good and evil, and Ralph's physical description puts him in opposition to the volatile Jack, and establishes him as a character who is morally upright and noble. Ralph's position as the hero is further cemented later in the novel when he shows courage; he announces his intention of climbing the mountain to see if there is a beast, stating that **'we'll go and look'**. The *declarative sentence* and the *modal verb* **'will'** work together to capture Ralph's clear sense of purpose. Even though he is frightened, Ralph still leads the boys up the mountain, demonstrating the traditional heroic quality of physical bravery.

☑ Move to the point that Golding presents Ralph as a leader

Ralph's position as a hero is reinforced when he quickly becomes leader of the boys, winning the vote to decide who becomes the chief. He is elected partly because he is defined by the boys as **'him with the shell'**. Ralph is linked with the conch which is used as a *symbol* of civilisation in the novel. Ralph becomes the democratically elected leader, ensuring that he is used to represent ordered society in the novel. Freudian analysis suggests that Ralph represents the 'ego', the part of us that struggles to resist our basic instincts and to comply with society's rules. Ralph's link with the conch reflects this stout-hearted desire to put society's needs before his own and indeed Golding describes him as having **'true leadership'**. From the beginning, he shows good instincts as a leader, representing the paternalistic aspects of government by making sensible decisions about shelters and latrines to make sure the community stays healthy and safe. Later in the novel, when Jack challenges Ralph's leadership, Golding continues to construct Ralph's character as one which represents civilised society. Ralph is aware of the importance of rules as the foundation of their society and passionately cries that **'the rules are the only thing we've got!'** The *exclamatory sentence* shows his passion; Ralph knows that the existence of their fragile society hangs on a knife edge and he is desperate to keep the community functioning. His *declarative sentence* reflects his valiant desire to cling to the remnants of society and civilisation as he remembers it. Golding uses Ralph and Jack to represent two schools of thought on how society should be run: Ralph represents democracy while Jack is moving towards a dictatorship. In this, Golding draws parallels with the recent World War 2, often viewed as a struggle between opposing ideologies.

☑ Make the point that Ralph does not always show heroic qualities

If Ralph is indeed the hero of the novel, he is certainly not a hero who is flawless. Ralph gets caught up in the taunting of Robert when the boys pretend that he is a pig and use him in a play-hunt which hovers on the edge of real violence: **'Ralph was fighting to get near, to get a handful of that brown, vulnerable flesh'**. Ralph does have a **'devil'** in him after all as he is attracted to the violence. The *repetitive clause* **'to get'** reflects his burning desire to hurt Robert. In the heat of the moment, Ralph does not see Robert as a frightened human; the *noun* **'flesh'** illustrates how Ralph has dehumanised Robert in his craving to overpower and inflict pain on him. Golding fought in World War 2 and saw even the best of men give in to savagery and brutality; Ralph's desire to hurt and kill is part of our nature and what Golding saw as the 'terrible disease' of being human. At the end, Ralph is hunted by the other boys and bursts out of his hiding place **'screaming, snarling, bloody'**. Far from a noble hero, Ralph is no more than a savage himself at the end. The *list* highlights this as he is inarticulately **'screaming'** and **'snarling'**. Language is one of the defining features of civilisation yet Ralph makes animal noises. Fear has reduced him to animal status as he is focused on no more than an instinctive will to survive; at this point, he seems far removed from any impression of a gallant, bold hero.

☑ Move to the point that there are other possible heroes in the novel

It is evident, then, that Ralph himself is not the noble hero we might expect; he is involved in the dreadful murder of Simon, showing that he is as capable of savage violence as the others and throwing into doubt his position as the hero of the story. There are also certainly other contenders for the title of hero in the novel. There is Piggy, who is the one who actually understands how to use the conch and instructs Ralph, knowing that the sound will call the others. It is Piggy who has the real knowledge and intelligence, not Ralph. Simon is also the possible hero with his pure qualities, his wise perception and his tragic death. Yet, according to literary conventions, Ralph is the hero of 'Lord of the Flies'. We see most events through his eyes and the novel follows his story, starting and ending with his experiences so that almost the last words of the book focus on Ralph as he **'wept for the end of innocence, the darkness of man's heart, and the fall through the air of the true, wise friend called Piggy'**. There is huge *pathos* in Ralph's tears as he understands how he has lost his childhood and witnessed unspeakable acts; the reader feels empathy with this central character and his desper-ate sadness. In this sense, the novel is a *bildungsroman*, a genre where the central character learns maturity. Ralph has learnt about the dark side of human nature and cannot forget this, returning to civilisation a changed character.

☑ Finish with an overview

In the pessimistic world of 'Lord of the Flies', Golding presents boys whose inner savagery is unleashed with dreadful consequences. While there are boys with heroic qualities, like Ralph, Golding's purpose was to explore the idea of the evil in humanity so it is unsurprising that there is no clear, indisputable hero of the novel.

2 Jack
Character analysis

Jack is the main antagonist of the novel whose desire for power and love of violence means that he challenges Ralph's democracy. Jack divides the community, leading his followers to become savage hunters that ends with the entire pack of boys chasing Ralph almost to his death.

'Eyes, frustrated now, turning, or ready to turn, to anger'

• Jack's eyes signal his short temper when he first meets Ralph.

• Golding uses the **motif** of eyes to explore ideas and characters. There is **foreshadowing** in the **motif**; Jack is presented as someone who will be hard to control and whose anger could well be linked to violence.

'We're not savages. We're English and the English are the best at everything'

• Jack agrees with Ralph that there should be rules on the island.

• His emphatic **declarative statements** reveal a nationalistic confidence. He is proud of his English heritage that marks him as superior to **'savages'**. He sees himself as civilised and morally sound and that, by being English, he is far removed from any primitive urges or savage instincts.

Context: Jack shows a patriotic pride that echoes back to colonial thinking when the British Empire stretched across the world and national confidence in the superiority of English society was firmly entrenched. Golding undermines any sense of English superiority; after all, immediately after Jack's confident statement, his fire burns out of control and kills the boy with the birthmark.

'strange invisible light of friendship, adventure and content'	• Jack and Ralph sit companionably in front of the fire they have jointly made. • The *metaphor* of light shows that Jack has the capacity to connect with others and enjoy the bonds of camaraderie. He is, like all humans, not born pure evil. • There is perhaps *foreshadowing* in the *adjective* **'strange'** which suggests that this bond of friendship is unusual and will not last.	**Context:** Golding subverts the genre of children's adventure books such as 'Coral Island' in which the children live outside the world of grown-ups and enjoy great camaraderie. Although the opening seems to suggest that the novel will fall into this genre, Golding twists it to reveal the bleak savagery at the heart of us all as the boys on the island violently turn on each other.
'the mask was a thing of its own, behind which Jack hid, liberated from shame'	• Jack paints his face in coloured mud, creating a mask. The mask allows Jack to explore his dark instincts which lead to violence. • The mask could reflect how civilisation itself is just a mask, covering our innate sense of evil. Once the mask of civilisation is taken off, human nature is seen to be violent and evil. Jack can now be himself and indulge in all his previously hidden desires to hurt.	**Context:** Golding uses Ralph and Jack to represent two schools of thought on how society should be run: Ralph represents democracy while Jack is moving towards a dictatorship. In this, Golding draws parallels with the recent World War 2, often viewed as a struggle between opposing ideologies.
'bollocks to the rules! We're strong - we hunt!'	• Jack dismisses the rules and the power of the conch. • Jack's use of the swear word **'bollocks'** illustrates just how much contempt he has for the rules of the community. At this point, Jack is realising that he can defy any regulations and follow his urges without any sanctions. • These urges are clear in the short, emphatic *clauses* **'we're strong! we hunt!'** which capture his powerful desire for violence.	**Context:** Using Freudian analysis, Jack represents the id, the side of our personalities which seeks to fulfill our own desires. 

> 'The chief was sitting there, naked to the waist... he pointed at this savage and that with his spear'

• Towards the end, Jack is in total control of his hunters.

• He has lost the name that links him to civilisation; instead of Jack, he is referred to as **'the chief'**.

• Golding uses clothing as a **motif** to illustrate the descent into savagery. At the start, Jack wore his chorister's cloak and cap but by the end is **'naked to the waist'**. As the community slips further into disorder, Jack's clothing becomes more sparse.

• His rule and power is based on violence; the way that he uses his spear to point at his followers reflects this.

Context: **Golding uses Jack and Ralph to represent two opposing ideologies: Jack represents an authoritarian leader. Jack is perhaps used as an *allegory* of Adolf Hitler; certainly, he is a dictator, allowing his followers no freedom and keeping power through fear and intimidation.**

Grade 9 Exploration:
Look at the character in a different way

At the end, do we have any sympathy left for Jack?

Yes: Jack is not a complete monster. The reader is uneasily aware that Jack is a young boy who has been put into an extraordinary situation which has allowed him to explore the darkness of his heart; we wonder just how far we would resist the temptations that the island presents and how easy we would find it to resist giving in to our primitive, savage urges. At the end, Ralph weeps and the **'other little boys'** join in. If Jack is included as one of these **'other little boys'**, then he too is overwhelmed by the knowledge of **'darkness of man's heart'**. He will return to civilisation as a boy who knows he has committed unspeakable acts.

Golding fought in World War 2 and saw even the best of men give in to brutality. Jack's desire to hurt and kill is part of human nature, common to us all.

No: Jack begins the novel as an unsympathetic character; even from the outset, he is described as **'something dark was fumbling along'** as the boys watch the choir draw closer. The dark imagery **foreshadows** Jack's savagery and certainly the first chapter establishes him as a cruel bully as he picks on Piggy and contemptuously orders the choir around. Golding places the reader to view most of the events of the novel from Ralph's point of view and, by the time Piggy is dead and we experience Ralph's frantic running to avoid Jack's murderous tribe, there is little or no sympathy for the vicious dictator who has completely given into his urges to hurt and kill.

Jack sees himself as civilised and morally sound and that, by being English, he is far removed from any primitive urges or savage instincts.

These urges are clear in the short, emphatic **clauses** which capture his desire for violence and reflects where he places value.

'We're not savages. We're English and the English are the best at everything'

'bollocks to the rules! We're strong- we hunt!'

Jack begins the novel agreeing to rules.

Jack begins to turn away from rules in order to satisfy his violent urges.

Jack

Jack fully descends into savagery.

Does the reader feel any sympathy for Jack?

'The chief was sitting there, naked to the waist… he pointed at this savage and that with his spear'

Yes: He is a young boy in an extraordinary situation and we wonder how easy we would find it to resist our primitive, savage urges in the same situation.

His rule and power is based on violence; the way that he uses his spear to point at his followers reflects this.

No: Even from the beginning, the foreboding **imagery** of **'something dark was fumbling along'** establishes Jack's innate savagery and love of violence.

Sample GCSE Exam Question

Q: How does Golding present Jack's descent into savagery in the novel?

 # Sample GCSE Answer

☑ Introduction: give an overview of the character

Golding presents the character of Jack as the main antagonist of the novel whose desire for power and love of violence means that he challenges Ralph's democracy. Jack divides the community, leading his followers to become savage hunters that ends with the entire pack of boys chasing Ralph almost to the death. Golding uses the character of Jack and his increasingly violent savagery to illustrate his message about **'mankind's essential illness'**: that we all have within us a capacity for evil.

☑ Start with the point that Jack begins the novel as a regular schoolboy

At the start of the novel, Jack is presented as a regular schoolboy who, just like the others, has been stranded on the island. He clearly attended a public school where he was head chorister and seems to uphold ideas of civilisation and order when he agrees with Ralph that there should be rules on the island, stating that **'we're not savages. We're English and the English are the best at everything'**. His emphatic *declarative statements* reveal a nationalistic confidence. He is proud of his English heritage that marks him as superior to **'savages'**. He sees himself as civilised and morally sound and that, by being English, he is far removed from any primitive urges or savage instincts. Jack's comments show a patriotic pride that echoes back to colonial thinking when the British Empire stretched across the world and national confidence in the superiority of English society was firmly entrenched. However, Golding deliberately undermines any sense of English superiority; after all, immediately after Jack's confident statement, his fire soon spreads out of control and kills the little boy with the birthmark, illustrating that their English heritage is not enough to keep the boys safe from violence. Yet there is a sense of optimism and excitement in the opening chapters as Jack and Ralph sit in front of the fire they have jointly made, pleased with their work and enjoying each other's company, surrounded by the **'strange invisible light of friendship, adventure and content'**. Golding celebrates the collaborative efforts that the boys have made through using a *metaphor* of light. The *list* of *nouns* captures the optimism that the boys still have in the early days on the island. They also highlight that Jack has the capacity to connect with others and enjoy the bonds of camaraderie. He is, like all humans, not born pure evil. There is perhaps *foreshadowing* in the *adjective* **'strange'** which suggests that this bond of friendship is unusual. Certainly, the friendships are soon torn apart as time wears on and attempts to conform to civilisation on the island break down. Golding subverts the genre of children's adventure books such as 'Coral Island' and 'Swallows & Amazons'. In these stories, the children live outside the world of grown-ups and enjoy great camaraderie and adventure throughout the novels until they are reunited with the adult world at the end. Yet Golding twists this genre to reveal the bleak savagery at the heart of us all as the boys on the island turn on each other, following their new leader, Jack.

☑ Move to the point that, even at the start, Golding shows us that Jack has a capacity for evil

This bleak savagery is hinted at from the beginning. Even in his initial description, Jack begins the novel as an unsympathetic character; from the outset, he is described as **'something dark was fumbling along'** as the boys watch the choir draw closer. The dark *imagery foreshadows* Jack's savagery and certainly the first chapter establishes him as a cruel bully as he picks on Piggy and contemptuously orders the choir around. Similarly, Golding uses the *motif* of eyes throughout the novel to reflect ideas and character and Jack's eyes are described as **'frustrated now, turning, or ready to turn, to anger'**. Jack is portrayed as a boy who is quick to anger and who has little self-control and, again, there is *foreshadowing* in the *motif*; Jack is presented as someone who will be hard to control and whose anger could well be linked to violence.

☑ Make the point that Jack soon begins to turn away from civilisation as his savage instincts become stronger

As the days pass on the island without any adult supervision, Jack's inner savagery begins to show itself. Jack paints his face in coloured mud, creating a mask that **'was a thing of its own, behind which Jack hid, liberated from shame and self-consciousness'**. The mask allows Jack to explore his dark instincts which lead him to violence. It ensures that he is **'liberated'**, free from the restraints that society places on behaviour. Alternatively, the mask could reflect how civilisation itself is just a mask, covering our innate sense of evil. Once the mask of civilisation is taken off, human nature is seen to be violent and evil. Jack can now be himself and indulge in all his previously hidden desires to hurt. William Golding believed that human nature is evil and that the boys are suffering from the 'terrible disease of being human'. As Jack moves further away from civilisation, he starts to succumb to this disease and eventually launches a challenge to Ralph's leadership: Ralph is aware of the importance of rules as the foundation of their society and states that **'the rules are the only thing we've got!'** but Jack dismisses these rules and the power of the conch when he answers with **'bollocks to the rules! We're strong- we hunt!'** Jack's use of the swear word **'bollocks'** reflects just how much contempt he has for the rules of the community. At this point, Jack is realising that he can defy any regulations and strictures and follow his urges without any sanctions. These urges are clear in the short, emphatic *clauses* **'we're strong!- we hunt!'** which capture his desire for violence and reflects where he places value. His values are not on rules and rational thought but on physical strength and blood lust, and the exclamation marks captures his forceful passion. Using Freudian analysis, Jack represents the id, the side of our personalities which seeks to fulfill our own desires. By rejecting the rules of civilisation, Jack is allowing the id to take precedence.

☑ Move to the point that, by the end of the novel, Jack's descent into savagery is complete

Towards the end, Jack is in total control of his hunters: **'The chief was sitting there, naked to the waist... he pointed at this savage and that with his spear'**. He is so far removed from the young chorister who arrived on the island that he has lost the name that links him to civilisation; instead of Jack, he is referred to as simply **'the chief'**. Golding uses clothing as a *motif* to reflect the descent into savagery. In the beginning, Jack wore his chorister's cloak and cap yet now, at the end, he is **'naked to the waist'**. As the community slips further into disorder, Jack's clothing becomes more sparse. His rule and power is based on violence; the way that he uses his spear to point at his followers reflects this. Golding uses Jack and Ralph to represent two opposing ideologies: Jack represents an authoritarian leader. Jack is perhaps used as an *allegory* of Adolf Hitler; certainly, he is a dictator, allowing his followers no freedom of action or freedom of speech. Yet Jack is not a complete monster. The reader is uneasily aware that Jack is a young boy who has been put into an extraordinary situation which has allowed him to explore the darkness of his heart; we wonder just how far we would resist the temptations that the island presents and how easy we would find it to resist giving in to our primitive, savage urges. At the end, Ralph weeps and the **'other little boys'** join in. If Jack is included as one of these **'other little boys'**, then he too is overwhelmed by the knowledge of **'darkness of man's heart'** that he has been so completely involved in. He will return to civilisation as a boy who knows he has committed unspeakable acts. Golding fought in World War 2 and saw even the best of men give in to savagery and brutality. Jack's desire to hurt and kill is part of human nature, common to us all.

☑ Finish with an overview

Whether we view Jack with any sympathy or not, it is evident that his character is used by Golding to illustrate just how easy it is for humans to succumb to their innate desire for violence. Golding places the reader to view most of the events of the novel from Ralph's point of view and, by the time Piggy is murdered and we experience Ralph's frantic running to avoid Jack's savage tribe, there is little doubt that Jack is stripped of any mask of civilisation and has fully given into his love of violence and brutality.

3 Piggy
Character analysis

Piggy is the overweight, short-sighted boy who helps Ralph create a community based on rules and democracy. As the boys descend into savagery, Piggy becomes ever more vulnerable until he is murdered near the end of the novel by the falling rock that is pushed by Roger.

'we can use this to call a meeting'

- Piggy understands how the conch can be used to summon the boys into one place.

- His words are sensible and pragmatic, understanding that there is a need to gather the boys in one place to begin to organise themselves.

- Yet, although he knows what to do with the conch, he does not take the conch from Ralph. Piggy is aware that he will be seen as inferior to the tall, charismatic Ralph. He is used to being put to one side.

Context: Golding uses Ralph and Jack to represent two opposing ideologies: Ralph represents democracy while Jack is interested in dictatorship. Golding uses the conch as a *symbol* of democracy in the novel; Piggy's association with conch links him to the powers of democracy.

'Piggy' 'Shut up, Fatty'

- Piggy is defined by his plump build and Jack enjoys mocking him about this.

- As laughter surrounds him, Piggy is established as a victim, as someone who is physically weaker and therefore open to abuse. His status as a figure of contempt and as an outsider is established.

- There is *foreshadowing* in Piggy's name and the bullying that he is subjected to; later, when the boys chant **'kill the pig!'**, there is a definite sense that they are truly wishing to kill Piggy, the weak outsider.

Context: Golding was a schoolteacher in a boys' school and saw first-hand the vicious taunting and bullying that went on among the children.

'like a crowd of kids'	• Piggy despairs of the way the boys rush off with no order or plans.

• Piggy detaches himself from the others and places himself alongside the absent grown-ups with their sensible, measured behaviour. Perhaps even at the beginning, Piggy knows that his very survival rests on the island's society being a community based on rules that will protect him. |

'Because what's right's right. Give me my glasses' 	• Piggy practises what he will say to Jack in order to get his stolen glasses back.

• There is determination and courage in these ***declarative sentences***.

• Piggy holds his moral position right until the end. He understands that stealing his glasses is fundamentally wrong and vehemently asserts this. | Context: **In Freudian analysis, Piggy is the super ego, the ethical part of us which tries to live by moral frameworks.** |

'exploded into a thousand white fragments'	• Piggy is killed as he holds the conch which **'exploded into a thousand white fragments'**.

• Piggy respects the values of free speech and rational thought right until the end. Yet this does not save him. With Piggy's death, the conch is shattered, ***symbolising*** the loss of order and reason on the island. | Context: **Golding fought in World War 2 and saw how violence and brutality consumed men. Piggy's death captures the viciousness and** |

> 'Ralph wept for the end of innocence, the darkness of man's heart, and the fall through the air of the true, wise friend called Piggy'

- At the end, Ralph acknowledges the value of his friendship with Piggy.

- The **adjectives** 'true' and **'wise'** show the reader the genuine nature of Piggy. Piggy was not physically brave or charismatic like Jack yet he is a much better friend and a much better person. Golding is perhaps suggesting to us that we need to adjust our values.

- There is huge **pathos** in Ralph's tears as he remembers his dead friend. **Structurally**, these are almost the last words of the novel. Golding ensures that Piggy is respected and honoured at the end.

Grade 9 Exploration:
Look at the character in a different way

Is Piggy the victim of class?

Yes: Piggy is marked as an outsider because of his speech which is grammatically incorrect. This immediately places him in a different social class to the other middle and upper class boys. He is at a disadvantage because of this; he speaks differently to the others and he also may well lack the confidence that the other boys will have had instilled in them through their privileged backgrounds.

Golding wrote 'Lord of the Flies' in the 1950s when society was more rigidly ordered by class that it is today. Piggy's lower social status immediately places him in a position of weakness.

No: Golding clearly states that **'Piggy was an outsider, not only by accent, which did not matter, but by fat'**. It is his physical shape which immediately marks him as a victim, not his social class.

Golding explores Darwinian ideas in the novel, showing how mankind has evolved through the survival of the fittest. Piggy's lack of physical strength means that he is vulnerable in the tough conditions of the island.

 # Essential Exam Tip

☑ Learn quotations off by heart. Write them out on sticky labels and put them in places where you go to all of the time e.g. the kettle or the bathroom mirror!

Piggy sees the practical use of the conch. Golding uses the conch as a *symbol* of democracy in the novel; Piggy's association with the conch links him to the powers of democracy.

Piggy generates hate and contempt; he is a vent for the boys' instinctive dark urges to hurt and humiliate.

'we can use this to call a meeting'

'Shut up, Fatty'

Piggy represents ordered society.

Piggy is bullied by the other boys.

Piggy

Piggy's death as he holds the conch *symbolises* the end to law and order.

Is Piggy the victim of class discrimination?

'exploded into a thousand white fragments'

Yes: Piggy is marked as an outsider because of his speech which is grammatically incorrect.

Golding fought in World War 2 and saw how violence and brutality consumed men. Piggy's death captures the viciousness and pointlessness of violence.

No: 'Piggy was an outsider, not only by accent, which did not matter, but by fat.' It is his physical shape which immediately marks him as a victim.

Sample GCSE Answer

☑ **Introduction:** give an overview of Piggy and his role in the novel

In Golding's novel 'Lord of the Flies', Piggy is the overweight, short-sighted school-boy who helps Ralph create a community based on rules and democracy. As the boys descend into savagery, Piggy becomes ever more vulnerable until he is murdered near the end of the novel by the falling rock that is pushed by Roger. Piggy is used as a **symbol** of the weak in society and Golding uses Piggy to illustrate how he becomes the victim of the other boys who are suffering from **'mankind's terrible illness'**, and to condemn the way that humankind treats the weak.

☑ **Start with the point that Piggy is presented as weak and vulnerable**

Piggy is defined by his plump build and Jack takes the first opportunity to mock him about this, telling him to **'shut up, Fatty'**. As laughter surrounds him, Piggy is immediately established as a victim, as someone who is physically weaker and therefore open to abuse. His status as a figure of contempt and as an outsider is established, and the boys overlook his many fine qualities simply because of his unattractive appearance. Piggy generates hate and contempt; he is a vent for the boys' instinctive dark urges to hurt and humiliate. There is **foreshadowing** in Piggy's name and the instant bullying that he is subjected to; later, when the boys chant **'kill the pig!'**, there is a definite sense that they are truly wishing to kill Piggy, the weakling, the outsider. The descent into savagery has begun, even in this first chapter. Golding was a schoolteacher in a boys' school and saw first-hand the vicious taunting and bullying that went on among the children. Piggy is marked as an outsider because of his speech which is grammatically incorrect. This immediately places him in a different social class to the other middle and upper class boys. He is at a disadvantage because of this; he speaks differently to the others and he also may well lack the confidence that the other boys will have had instilled in them through their privileged backgrounds. Golding wrote 'Lord of the Flies' in the 1950s when society was more rigidly ordered by class that it is today. Piggy's lower social status immediately places him in a position of weakness yet Golding clearly states that **'Piggy was an outsider, not only by accent, which did not matter, but by fat'**. It is his physical shape which immediately marks him as a victim, not his social class. Golding explores Darwinian ideas in the novel, showing how mankind has evolved through the survival of the fittest. Piggy's lack of physical strength means that he is vulnerable in the tough conditions of the island, and we worry from the outset that he will suffer.

☑ **Move to the point that Piggy is linked to democracy**

Yet Piggy is not just used as a symbol of the weak in society. Piggy is a boy of logic and rationality, understanding how the conch can be used to summon the separated boys into one place: **'we can use this to call a meeting'**. His words are sensible and pragmatic, understanding that there is a need to gather the boys in one place to begin to organise themselves. While Ralph is transfixed by the conch's beauty, Piggy sees the practical use of the conch. Golding uses the conch as a **symbol** of democracy in the novel and Piggy is associated from the beginning with the conch and therefore with the powers of democracy. Yet, although he knows what to do with the conch, he does not take the conch from Ralph. Piggy is aware that he will be seen as inferior to the tall, charismatic Ralph. He is used to being put to one side. Golding uses Ralph and Jack to represent two opposing ideologies: Ralph represents democracy while Jack is drawn to dictatorship. With his close association with the conch, Piggy is firmly linked to these ideas of democracy.

✔ Make the point that Piggy is a symbol of logical thought

Piggy is also established as a sensible, logical boy when he despairs of the way the boys rush off with no order or plans, behaving **'like a crowd of kids'**. He detaches himself from the others and places himself alongside the absent grown-ups with their sensible, measured behaviour. Perhaps even at the beginning, Piggy knows that his very survival rests on the island's society being a community based on rules that will protect him. Yet, ironically, it is partly because of this mature behaviour which is more suited to an adult than a school boy that sets him apart from the others and makes him such a target. The word **'crowd'** shows that the boys are already acting in a pack mentality, perhaps a reference to the mob mentality that Hitler tapped into so successfully in Nazi Germany. Piggy's role as a representation of rational thought is also cemented through the *symbolism* of his glasses which reflect the power of science. He relies on them and at the end, he practises what he will say to Jack in order to get his stolen glasses back: **'because what's right's right. Give me my glasses.'** There is determination and courage in these *declarative sentences*. Even though Piggy has been left even more vulnerable through the loss of his glasses, he is resolved to confront the terror that Jack has become. Piggy holds his moral position right until the end, understanding that stealing his glasses is fundamentally wrong and vehemently asserts this; indeed, in Freudian analysis, Piggy is the super ego, the ethical part of us which tries to live by moral frameworks. It is possible that Golding mocks the logical, rational Piggy as Piggy relies heavily on scientific explanations to rationalise events on the island and admires the capabilities of science and technology: **'life,' said Piggy expansively, 'is scientific, that's what it is. In a year or two when the war's over they'll be travelling to Mars and back'**. However, the boys are stranded on the island as a direct result of the power of science and the atomic bomb which is tearing the world apart, and so Golding undercuts Piggy's appreciative words. Golding lived in the dawn of the atomic age and the fear of nuclear war, and uses the novel and Piggy to illustrate that humankind uses science for terrible ends.

✔ Move to the end of the novel and Piggy's death

Although it is possible that Golding sometimes mocks Piggy, there is nothing but *pathos* at the end when Piggy is killed as he holds the conch which **'exploded into a thousand white fragments'**. Piggy respects the values of free speech and rational thought right until the end yet this does not save him. With Piggy's death, the conch is shattered, symbolising the loss of order and reason on the island. The violence of Piggy's death is caught in the powerful *verb* **'exploded'** and the utter destruction of the conch into a **'thousand white fragments'**. Golding fought in World War 2 and saw how violence and brutality consumed men, and Piggy's death is a dramatic, painful example of this savagery. At the end, Ralph acknowledges the value of his friendship with Piggy as he **'wept for the end of innocence, the darkness of man's heart, and the fall through the air of the true, wise friend called Piggy.'** The *adjectives* **'true'** and **'wise'** show the reader the genuine nature of Piggy. Piggy was not physically brave or charismatic like Jack yet he is a much better friend and a much better person. Golding is perhaps showing us that we need to adjust our values. There is a huge pathos in Ralph's tears as he remembers his dead friend. *Structurally*, these are almost the last words of the novel and so Golding ensures that Piggy is respected and honoured at the end.

✔ Finish with an overview

Piggy is an integral part of 'Lord of the Flies', fulfilling a number of roles. He represents logical thought and democracy yet it is perhaps his vulnerability that the reader remembers him for. Golding uses Piggy and the way that he is relentlessly bullied to illustrate how the weak are abused by the strong and how humankind needs to be aware of how savagery and evil must be resisted.

4 Simon
Character analysis

Simon is the unusual boy who stands apart from the rest of the boys. He is the one who realises that the evil on the island comes from within the boys themselves but is murdered before he can share this knowledge.

'smiled pallidly'

- Simon is physically different to the other boys as he faints and **'smiled pallidly'**.

- The **adverb 'pallidly'** reveals that his smile is dull as he recovers from his faint. His weakness marks him out as different from the others.

- Simon represents human goodness. His physical weakness **foreshadows** how goodness will be overcome by the savagery that is later unleashed.

'pulled off the choicest' (fruit)

- Simon takes fruit from the trees to give to the littluns.

- Simon's innate kindness and generosity is shown in his actions, taking the time to help feed the weaker littluns. His selflessness is shown in the **superlative adjective 'choicest'**, emphasising how he gives the best fruit to the others rather than keeping it for himself.

- Simon works to help the others, revealing a collaborative approach that Golding approved of.

Context: In Freudian analysis, Simon represents the superego. This is the part of us which aspires to idealistic moral values and Simon's behaviour reflects this.

'candle-like buds'

- Simon withdraws into the forest to be alone with nature. Simon finds a peaceful, beautiful place where it is quiet and serene; the *imagery* of the buds being **'candle-like'** helps create an atmosphere of a church or a temple.

- Simon retreats from the boys' company to be at one with nature, reflecting his spiritual nature. He has a perception and thoughtfulness that set him out as an outsider.

Context: Golding possibly uses Lord of the Flies to present a religious *allegory* with the boys in a Garden of Eden and then falling into sin. Simon's withdrawal from society and his links with **'candle-like buds'** establish him as the Christ figure in this *allegory*.

'I'm part of you. Close, close, close!'

- It is Simon who realises that evil is an intrinsic part of human nature as he talks to the Lord of the Flies.

- There is a sense of *foreshadowing* in the *repetition* of the words **'close'**; each time, the Lord of the Flies reminds Simon just how fragile the veneer of civilisation is. Simon has the perception to see that the beast is inside us all, and to recognise the darkness of man's heart.

'The dark sky was shattered by a blue white scar'

- Simon is killed in the middle of a storm.

- Golding uses the storm to reveal the violent horror of Simon's death. Simon is seen as having an affinity with nature so this disruption of nature in the use of a storm reflects the brutality of his death.

'Kill the beast! Cut his throat! Spill his blood!'

- The boys kill Simon in a frenzy of blood-lust.

- There is a sacrificial element to Simon's death, again reflecting his association with Christ who was murdered by his own people.

- Simon's death marks a changing point in the novel. The boys' descent into savagery is now unstoppable; by killing Simon, who embodies goodness, they are now free to unleash the darkness within them.

Grade 9 Exploration:
Look at the character in a different way

Is Simon a *symbol* rather than a 'real' character?

Yes: Golding's portrayal of Simon is unrealistic; his selflessness and spirituality ensures that he is not depicted as a 'real' boy. He **symbolises** goodness and perception which is unachievable and so Simon's

No: Although he is an outsider, Simon is more than a **symbol**. Like the other boys, he is excited by the adventure of being on the island and play-fights with Ralph and Jack so that the three boys roll around in a **'happy, heaving pile'**. Simon readily fits into this romping group. Furthermore, his kindness and perception are human qualities.

At first, 'Lord of the Flies' seems to fit the genre of castaway novels such as 'Coral Island' and 'Swallows and Amazons' with Simon and the others excitedly exploring the island. Yet Golding subverts the genre; by the time Simon is hacked to death, the boys have left behind any jolly adventuring and show they are more than capable of bloody murder.

 # Essential Exam Tip

☑ Most of the exam boards require you to write about context but it does differ. Some exam boards will be looking for lots of contextual points while others won't be assessing it at all. Check what your exam board specifies.

Simon helps the littluns to the best fruit, illustrating how he is selfless and kind.

Simon realises that evil is part of all of us as he talks to the Lord of the Flies.

'pulled off the choicest (fruit)'

'I'm part of you. Close, close, close!'

Simon embodies goodness.

Simon understands human nature.

Simon

Simon's death marks a changing point in the novel.

Is Simon a *symbol*?

'Kill the beast! Cut his throat! Spill his blood!'

Yes: The portrayal of Simon is unrealistic. He is not a 'real' boy, more a *symbol* of goodness and perception.

There is a sacrificial element to Simon's death, reflecting his association with Christ who was murdered by his own people.

No: He is a normal little boy, excited by the adventure of being on the island and play-fighting with Ralph and Jack so that the three boys roll around in a **'happy, heaving pile'**.

Sample GCSE Exam Question

Q: What is the importance of the character of Simon in 'Lord of the Flies'?

 # Sample GCSE Answer

☑ Introduction: start with an overview of Simon

In the dystopian world of 'Lord of the Flies', Simon is the unusual boy who stands apart from the rest of the boys. He is the one who realises that the evil on the island comes from within the boys themselves and it is painfully ironic that he is killed by them just at the moment he is about to share this knowledge. Golding uses the character of Simon to explore ideas of good and evil within human nature.

☑ Start with the point that Simon is important because he represents goodness

Simon is physically different to the other boys as he faints and then **'smiled pallidly'**. The **adverb 'pallidly'** tells us that his smile is dull as he recovers from his faint. His weakness marks him out as different from the others and so Golding constructs Simon as a character who is an outsider. Simon represents human goodness and his physical weakness **foreshadows** how goodness will be overcome by the savagery that is later unleashed. This goodness is illustrated when Simon takes fruit from the trees to give to the littluns; he **'pulled off the choicest'** fruit for them. His innate kindness and generosity is shown in his actions, taking the time to help feed the weaker littluns. His selflessness is captured in the **superlative adjective 'choicest'** which emphasises how he gives the best fruit to the others rather than keeping it for himself, revealing a collaborative approach that Golding approved of. In Freudian analysis, Simon represents the superego. This is the part of us which aspires to idealistic moral values and Simon's behaviour reflects this as he puts his own needs to one side and places the little boys' needs as a higher priority. Simon's goodness is further established through his solitude and thoughtfulness when he retreats from the boys' company to be at one with nature, reflecting his spiritual nature. He withdraws into the forest to be alone, finding a quiet spot where he sits reflecting amongst **'candle-like buds'**. He chooses a peaceful, beautiful place where it is quiet and serene; the **imagery** of the buds being **'candle-like'** helps create an atmosphere of a church or a temple. Golding possibly uses Lord of the Flies to present a religious **allegory** with the boys in a Garden of Eden and then falling into sin. Simon's withdrawal from society and his links with **'candle-like buds'** establish him as the Christ figure in this **allegory**, someone who is pure and good.

☑ Make the point that Simon is important because he understands the nature of evil

It is not just his morality that marks Simon out as different; his perception and thoughtfulness also separates him from the other boys. It is Simon who realises that the evil is an intrinsic part of human nature as he communicates with the Lord of the Flies who tells him that **'I'm part of you. Close, close, close!'** There is a sense of **foreshadowing** in the **repetition** of the words

'close'; each time, the Lord of the Flies reminds Simon just how fragile the human conscience is and therefore how fragile the veneer of civilisation is. Simon has the perception to see that the Beast is inside us all, and to recognise the darkness of man's heart that Golding called 'the terrible disease of being human'. Golding uses Simon to convey this idea that evil is part of us. Having fought in the recent World War 2, Golding was painfully aware of how savage instincts lie just under the veneer of civilisation and used the boys on the island to explore this.

☑ Move to the point that Simon's death is important

This savagery is first truly demonstrated through Simon's death. It is ironic that Simon is mistaken for the beast and killed at the moment when he is trying to tell the boys that there is no such thing. Simon's murder takes place in the middle of a storm as **'the dark sky was shattered by a blue white scar'**. Golding uses the weather to reveal the violent horror of Simon's death. Simon is seen as having an affinity with nature so this disruption of nature in the use of a storm reflects the brutality of his death. This brutality is captured through the boys' frenzied chanting of **'kill the beast! Cut his throat! Spill his blood!'** The *monosyllabic* words and the vicious *imperative verbs* at the start of each stark sentence capture the blood-frenzied mentality that has completely overtaken the boys. There is a sacrificial element to Simon's death, as violent and barbaric as Christ's death, again reflecting his association with Christ who was murdered by his own people. Simon's death marks a changing point in the novel. The boys' descent into savagery is now unstoppable; by killing Simon, who embodies goodness and wisdom, they are now free to unleash the darkness within them.

☑ Explore how Golding uses him as a *symbol*

It could certainly appear that Golding's portrayal of Simon is unrealistic; Simon's selflessness and spirituality ensures that he is not a 'real' boy. He **symbolises** a goodness and perception which is unachievable and so Simon's importance in the novel is that of a **symbol**. However, although he is an outsider and a representation of essential goodness, Simon is more than a **symbol**. Like the other boys, he is excited by the adventure of being on the island and play-fights with Ralph and Jack so that the three boys roll around in a **'happy, heaving pile'**. Simon readily fits into this romping group and at first, 'Lord of the Flies' seems to fit the genre of castaway novels such as 'Coral Island' and 'Swallows and Amazons' with Simon and the others excitedly exploring the island. Yet Golding subverts the genre; by the time Simon is hacked to death, the boys have left behind any jolly adventuring and show they are more than capable of bloody murder. The reader feels the *pathos* of Simon's unnecessary and horrific death, and mourns for the loss of this sweet, pure boy.

☑ Finish with an overview

Golding constructs a character who understands and presents the underlying message of his fable: that mankind has an **'essential illness'**, that of the desire to do evil if given the opportunity. Simon's perception in comprehending this message sets him apart from the others and, perhaps as a result, he is slaughtered by the others. Through his presentation of Simon's goodness and unjust death, Golding encourages us to reject our own inner savagery and hold firm onto our own goodness.

Roger is the quiet, secretive boy who wields violence as a tool for power and for pure enjoyment. Golding uses Roger to help demonstrate the desire for violence that lies within us all.

'vision of red and yellow... witch-like cry'

- A bird makes a sound which is a **'witch-like cry'**.

- The island is a place of great beauty; the bird is described as a **'vision of red and yellow'** but it also has a **'witch-like cry'**. The *simile* suggests that the bird is evil with unpleasant intentions, perhaps *foreshadowing* the horrors that the boys will experience.

- The island is therefore established as a place of ambiguity and potential violence and this is unsettling for the boys and for the readers.

Context: Golding created an island setting where the boys are confined in order to explore ideas about human nature when civilisation is left behind. He fought in World War Two and saw even the best of men give in to savagery and brutality. His novel probes the dark violent nature of man, what Golding described as the 'terrible disease' of being human, and the isolated island setting acts as a microcosm of the real world to help explore this theme.

'kept to himself with an inner intensity of avoidance and secrecy'

- Roger is a quiet, withdrawn boy. He separates himself from the rest of the group. Roger's isolation and **'intensity'** makes the reader slightly uneasy. His position as an outsider forewarns us that he might act outside the boundaries of 'civilised' society.

'Roger's arm was conditioned by a civilisation that knew nothing of him and was in ruins'

- Roger throws stones at the littleuns but holds back from hurting them with a direct aim. His arm is **'conditioned'** not to hurt the littluns, implying that kindness and a desire to protect is not part of our human nature. These elements are taught to us by society and **'civilisation'**. It is violence that comes naturally to us.

- Yet violence also comes to civilisation; the world of adults and civilised behaviour was **'in ruins'**, destroyed by an atomic bomb.

- **Structurally**, this episode is important as Roger moves closer to hurting the other children. The reader sees how civilisation '**knew nothing of him'** and so Roger will soon realise this and be free of its rules and restrictions that are the only thing that prevents him from violence.

Context: The end of World War Two was marked by the dropping of atomic bombs on Japan. The fear of nuclear war was a constant threat in the post-war world; in the novel, Golding uses this contemporary idea of a world caught up in an atomic war as a background to the plot.

'Kill the beast! Cut his throat!'

- The boys kill Simon in a frenzy of blood-lust.

- The chant illustrates the mob mentality that consumes the boys. The **monosyllabic** words and the **imperative verbs** create a chilling sense of vicious violence.

- Simon's death marks a changing point in the novel. The boys' descent into savagery is now unstoppable; by killing Simon, who embodies goodness, they are now free to unleash the darkness and violence within them.

| 'exploded into a thousand white fragments' | • Roger pushes the rock that kills Piggy and smashes the conch which **"exploded into a thousand white fragments"**.

• Piggy respects the values of free speech and rational thought right until the end. Yet this does not save him from the forces of violence. With Piggy's death, the conch is shattered, **symbolising** the loss of order and reason on the island. While there was a bloodlust surrounding the killing of Simon, Piggy's death was very deliberate. Roger precisely pushes the rock which kills Piggy and smashes the conch. Violence now rules on the island. |

Grade 9 Exploration:
Look at the theme in a different way

Does the ending show us that violence has been expunged?

Yes: At the end, the violence is over and **'Ralph wept for the end of innocence, the darkness of man's heart, and the fall through the air of the true, wise friend called Piggy'**. There is a huge **pathos** in Ralph's tears as he sees how he has lost his childhood and witnessed unspeakable acts; the reader feels empathy with this central character and perhaps feels that lessons have been learnt about how to reject the desire for violence that lies within us.

No: Ralph is saved by a naval officer who is equipped with **'white drill, epaulettes, a revolver'**. It is only organised violence in the shape of the military that saves Ralph from death, reminding us that in the adult world, it is those who can command violent forces who hold power. The officer is oblivious to the real dynamics of the group of boys, comparing them to 'Coral Island'. It seems that humankind's desire for violence is an innate part of us and can never be fully suppressed.

Golding subverts the genre of children's adventure books such as 'Coral Island' and 'Swallows and Amazons'. In these stories, the children live outside the world of grown-ups and enjoy great camaraderie and adventure throughout the novels until they are reunited with the adult world at the end. Yet Golding twists this genre to show the bleak savagery at the heart of us all as the boys on the island violently turn on each other.

 # Essential Exam Tip

☑ Start revising for the exams early. Revising in ten minute bursts from the end of Year 10 can make a huge difference and reduces the last minute panic before your exams.

Roger's isolation and **'intensity'** makes the reader slightly uneasy. His position as an outsider forewarns us that he might act outside the boundaries of 'civilised' society.

The chant illustrates the mob mentality that consumes the boys.

'kept to himself with an inner intensity of avoidance and secrecy'

'Kill the beast! Cut his throat!'

Roger is an outsider with a propensity for violence.

We all have within us a desire for violence.

Roger & Violence

Violence triumphs over civilisation.

Does the ending show us that violence has been expunged?

'exploded into a thousand white fragments'

Yes: Lessons have been learnt by the end of the novel. Through awareness and understanding, we can tame our desires to hurt and maim.

With Piggy's brutal death, the conch is shattered, *symbolising* the loss of order and reason on the island.

No: Ralph is saved by a naval officer who is equipped with **'white drill, epaulettes, a revolver'**. It is only organised violence in the shape of the military that saves Ralph from death.

Sample GCSE Exam Question

Q: How is the theme of violence presented in 'Lord of the Flies'?

Sample GCSE Answer

☑ Introduction: start with an overview of the theme of violence

Golding used 'Lord of the Flies' to explore his belief that all humans have a capacity for evil and violence. He believed that the restraints of society force us to behave in a morally good way but, if these restraints are stripped away then, in the end, savagery will win over civilisation and humans will commit terrible, evil acts. The characters and the plot of the novel are carefully constructed to explore this idea of how our desire for violence can overpower us.

☑ Make the point that there are hints of violence from the opening chapters

The opening chapters seem at first to follow the genre of children's adventure stories such as 'Coral Island' and 'Swallows and Amazons'. In these stories, the children live outside the world of grown-ups and enjoy great camaraderie and adventure throughout the novels until they are reunited with the adult world at the end. The boys are alone on the island which is a place of great beauty; for example, there is a bird which is described as a **'vision of red and yellow'**. It is stunning yet it also has a **'witch-like cry'**. The *simile* suggests that the bird is evil with unpleasant intentions, perhaps *foreshadowing* the horrors that the boys will experience. The island is therefore established as a place of ambiguity and potential violence and this is unsettling for the boys and for the readers. Golding created an island *setting* where the boys are confined in order to explore ideas about human nature when civilisation is left behind. He fought in World War Two and saw even the best of men give in to savagery and brutality. His novel probes the dark violent nature of man, what Golding described as the 'terrible disease' of being human, and the isolated island *setting* acts as a microcosm of the real world to help explore this theme.

☑ Continue this point that there are warnings of violence from the opening

Golding uses characters as well to explore ideas of violence, in particular the character of Roger. Roger is a quiet, withdrawn boy who **'kept to himself with an inner intensity of avoidance and secrecy'**. He separates himself from the rest of the group and his isolation and **'intensity'** work with the island *setting* to make the reader slightly uneasy. Roger's position as an outsider forewarns us that he might act outside the boundaries of 'civilised' society. Certainly, he is the boy who seems to most easily give in to his desire to inflict pain. Before long, the reader sees evidence of this as Roger begins to throw stones at the littluns but holds back from hurting them with a direct aim. His arm **'was conditioned by a civilisation that knew nothing of him and was in ruins'** not to hurt the littluns. This **'condition(ing)'** implies that kindness and a desire to protect is not part of our human nature. These elements are taught to us by society and **'civilisation'**, and it is violence that comes naturally to us. Yet, interestingly, violence also comes to civilisation; the world of adults and civilised behaviour was **'in ruins'**, destroyed by an atomic bomb. The end of World War Two was marked by the dropping of atomic bombs on Japan. The fear of nuclear war was a constant threat in the post-war world; in the novel, Golding uses this contemporary idea of a world caught up in an atomic war as a background to the plot.

☑ Move to the point that, as time passes, the boys' desire for violence begins to drive the plot

As time passes, the civilised world seems to recede ever further from the boys' memories and the descent into savagery begins in earnest. The boys kill Simon in a frenzy of blood-lust, chanting **'kill the beast! Cut his throat! Spill his blood!'** The chant illustrates the mob mentality that has consumed the boys and the ***monosyllabic words*** and the ***imperative verbs*** create a chilling sense of vicious violence. Simon's death marks a changing point in the novel. The boys' descent into savagery is now unstoppable; by killing Simon, who embodies goodness, they are now free to unleash the darkness and violence within them. The violence becomes more prominent and more brutal, leading to the moment where Roger pushes the rock that kills Piggy and smashes the conch which **'exploded into a thousand white fragments'**. While there was a crazed bloodlust surrounding the killing of Simon, Piggy's death is very deliberate. It is Roger who precisely pushes the rock which kills Piggy and smashes the conch. He is now far from the **'condition(ing)'** influence of society and is free to explore his inner desire to hurt, maim and kill. With Piggy's death, the conch is shattered, ***symbolising*** the loss of order and reason on the island. Violence now rules on the island. This violence is caught in the powerful ***verb 'exploded'*** and the utter destruction of the conch into a **'thousand white fragments'**.

☑ Explore the point whether violence has been expunged by the end of the novel

Golding does, perhaps, allow us some hope that lessons have been learned and that violence has been reined in by the end. At the end, the violence is over and **'Ralph wept for the end of innocence, the darkness of man's heart, and the fall through the air of the true, wise friend called Piggy'**. There is a huge ***pathos*** in Ralph's tears as he sees how he has lost his childhood and witnessed unspeakable acts; the reader feels empathy with this central character and his desperate sadness. Through awareness and understanding, we can tame our desires to hurt and maim. Yet this is perhaps overly optimistic. Ralph is saved by a naval officer who is equipped with **'white drill, epaulettes, a revolver'**. It is only organised violence in the shape of the military that saves Ralph from death reminding us that in the adult world, it is those who can command violent forces who hold power. The officer is oblivious to the real dynamics of the group of boys, comparing them to 'Coral Island', and indeed Golding subverts this genre of children's adventure books such as 'Coral Island' by showing the bleak savagery at the heart of us all as the boys on the island violently turn on each other in a way which would most certainly have ended in their death but by chance.

☑ Finish with an overview

'Lord of the Flies' illustrates the violence that lies within all of us and uncompromisingly shows us how it takes very little for us to unleash our own inner dark savagery.

6 Sam & Eric
Character analysis

Sam and Eric are identical twins who are initially loyal to Ralph but are overwhelmed by the savagery of the tribe and betray him.

'flung themselves down and lay grinning'	• Sam and Eric begin the novel as cheerful, happy boys. • The **verb 'flung'** reflects their youthful energy and the **verb 'grinning'** captures their pleasure in the situation. The reader sees how they are full of enthusiasm for the island and all the fun and adventure it offers them.	**Context:** Golding subverts the genre of children's adventure books such as 'Coral Island' and 'Swallows & Amazons'. In these stories, the children live outside the world of grown-ups and enjoy great camaraderie and adventure throughout the novels until they are reunited with the adult world at the end. Yet Golding twists this genre to expose the bleak savagery at the heart of us all as the boys on the island violently turn on each other.

'lay grinning and panting at Ralph like dogs' 	• The twins are compared to dogs. • The **simile** captures their loyalty to Ralph who already seems to be the leader of the boys. This instant devotion to Ralph establishes the boys as representations of the ordinary members of the public who are happy to abide by whichever authority is in charge.	**Context:** Golding wrote 'Lord of the Flies' just after World War Two. He perhaps uses Sam and Eric to represent the ordinary people in Nazi Germany who showed unquestioning obedience and so allowed the rise of Hitler.

'They breathed together, they grinned together' 'Samneric'

- The twins are constantly linked as one entity.

- The **repeated** sentence structure highlights how the boys are constantly seen as a pair.

- Golding uses the boys to explore the idea of the individual versus the collective. In the beginning, the boys are individuals with a sense of self and personal responsibility. Sam and Eric have always been part of a pair so this sense of self will always have been less defined.

- As the novel progresses, the twins are used by Golding to show how the boys are losing their sense of individuality as they form tribes and hunt in packs. The blurring of Sam and Eric into one name- **'Samneric'** - reflects this shift.

'we left early'

- The twins participate in the murder of Simon but then deny all knowledge.

- They are capable of dreadful violence, just like we all are.

Context: In Freudian analysis, Sam and Eric are like Ralph and Piggy who fit into the concept of the ego. The twins want to do what is right yet they are also drawn to the id, the part of us which is primitive and aggressive. Their participation in the murder reflects this.

- When the twins are captured by Jack's tribe, Samneric try to resist.

- Golding uses the twins to reflect the power of evil and violence. The short, **exclamatory sentences** use mild language yet there is a world of fear and pain behind them as the tribe throws them to the ground.

Context: Golding fought in World War Two and saw how violence and brutality consumed men. William Golding believed that human nature is evil and that we all suffer from the 'terrible disease of being human'. Sam and Eric might protest from the **'heart of civilisation'** yet it does not help them as violence and savagery have taken control.

Grade 9 Exploration:
Look at the character in a different way

Do Sam and Eric provide comic relief in the novel?

Yes: The twins are endearing characters and some of their interactions help provide much needed comic relief in a novel full of horror and violence. An example of this is when they mimic their irate schoolteacher while they are on fire duty, giggling as they recall his shouts: **'Boy -you- are- driving -me- slowly -insane!'** Another example is Sam's rueful honesty when the hunters steal Piggy's glasses; dissecting the fight, Sam's brave claim that **'we gave them something to think about'** is soon changed to **'at least you did. I got myself mixed up with myself in a corner.'** The idea of Sam violently fighting with himself and then his endearing honesty about this provides the reader with some light-hearted moments.

No: Any comic relief is undercut by the actions of the twins. Golding shows the descent into violence even in the twins, whose cheerful, amiable personalities have been a constant throughout the novel. Near the end, the twins are **'locked in an embrace, fighting each other'** but this is not entertaining; it is horrific and indicative of the terrible savagery that the boys have unleashed in themselves. If Sam and Eric, the identical twins, are violent to one another, there is little hope that the other boys will be able to resist their brutal urges. Their fighting is not funny; it is tragic.

Golding possibly uses 'Lord of the Flies' to present a religious *allegory* with the boys in a Garden of Eden and then falling into sin. The two fighting brothers are representative of Cain and Abel from the Bible and remind us of how we are doomed to violence.

This instant devotion to Ralph establishes the boys as representations of the ordinary members of the public who are happy to abide by whichever authority is in charge.

As the novel progresses, the boys begin to lose their sense of individuality as they form tribes. The blurring of Sam and Eric into one name reflects this.

'lay grinning and panting at Ralph like dogs'

Samneric

Sam and Eric are loyal to Ralph.

Sam and Eric reflect ideas of the individual versus the collective.

Sam and Eric

Their treatment reflects the power of violence.

Do Sam and Eric provide comic relief in the novel?

'Protested out of the heart of civilisation, 'Oh, I say!' 'Honestly'

Yes: The twins' endearing personalities provide much needed comic relief; imitating their school teacher and their fighting later in the novel are light-hearted moments.

Their cries highlight the terrible power of violence. The short *exclamatory sentences* convey a world of terror and pain.

No: Their fighting is tragic; if the identical twins can fight each other, then there is no hope that the other boys will be able to resist their brutal urges.

Q: How does Golding use Sam and Eric to present the themes of the novel?

 Sample GCSE Answer

✓ Introduction: start with an overview of the characters

In the dystopian novel, 'Lord of the Flies', Sam and Eric are identical twins who are initially loyal to Ralph but are overwhelmed by the savagery of the tribe and betray him. Golding uses Sam and Eric to explore different themes such as individual responsibility and how humankind is drawn to violence and savagery.

✓ Start with the point that Sam and Eric represent ordinary boys

Sam and Eric begin the novel as cheerful, happy boys, joining the group of boys where they **'flung themselves down and lay grinning'**. The *verb* **'flung'** captures their youthful energy and the *verb* **'grinning'** reflects their pleasure in the situation. The reader sees how they are full of enthusiasm for the island and all the fun and adventure it offers them. Golding subverts the genre of children's adventure books such as 'Coral Island' and 'Swallows & Amazons'. In these stories, the children live outside the world of grown-ups and enjoy great camaraderie and adventure throughout the novels until they are reunited with the adult world at the end. Yet Golding twists this genre to show the bleak savagery at the heart of us all as the boys on the island violently turn on each other; Sam and Eric's initial enthusiasm will turn to pain and terror. Yet at the start they **'lay grinning and panting at Ralph like dogs'**. The *simile* compares the twins to dogs which reflects their loyalty to Ralph who already seems to be the leader of the boys. This instant devotion to Ralph establishes the boys as representations of the ordinary members of the public who are happy to abide by whichever authority is in charge. Golding wrote 'Lord of the Flies' just after World War 2. He perhaps uses Sam and Eric to represent the ordinary people in Nazi Germany who showed unquestioning obedience and so allowed the rise of Hitler.

✓ Move to the point that Golding uses them to explore ideas of individuality versus the collective

The twins are constantly linked as one entity, for example **'they breathed together, they grinned together'**. The *repeated* sentence structure highlights how the boys are constantly seen as a pair. Golding uses the boys to explore the idea of the individual versus the collective. In the beginning, all of the boys are individuals with a sense of self and personal responsibility. Sam and Eric have always been part of a pair so this sense of self will always have been less defined. As the novel progresses, the twins are used by Golding to show how the boys are losing their sense of individuality as they form tribes and hunt in packs. The blurring of Sam and

Eric into one name, **'Samneric'**, reflects this shift. The twins participate in the murder of Simon but then deny all knowledge, reflecting how they act as part of a group but deny individual responsibility for their actions, saying that **'we left early'**. They are capable of dreadful violence, just like we all are. Golding uses the novel to explore **'mankind's essential illness'**, our inner desire for violence. In Freudian analysis, Sam and Eric are like Ralph and Piggy who fit into the concept of the ego. The twins want to do what is right yet they are also drawn to the id, the part of us which is primitive and aggressive. Their participation in the murder shows this.

☑ Make the point that the boys help illustrate the descent into savagery

Golding uses the twins to reflect the power of evil and violence. When the twins are captured by Jack's tribe, Samneric try to resist; they **'protested out of the heart of civilisation. "Oh, I say!" " —Honestly!"** The short, *exclamatory sentences* use mild language yet there is a world of fear and pain behind them as the tribe takes control of the twins, throwing them to the ground. Golding fought in World War Two and saw how violence and brutality consumed men. William Golding believed that human nature is evil and that we all suffer from the 'terrible disease of being human'. Sam and Eric might protest from the **'heart of civilisation'** yet it does not help them as violence and savagery have taken control.

☑ Explore whether Sam and Eric provide comic relief in the novel

The twins are endearing characters and some of their interactions help provided much needed comic relief in a novel full of horror and violence. An example of this is when they mimic their irate schoolteacher while they are on fire duty, giggling as they recall his shouts: **'boy -you-are- driving -me- slowly -insane!'** Another example is Sam's rueful honesty when the hunters steal Piggy's glasses; dissecting the fight, Sam's brave claim that **'we gave them something to think about'** is soon changed to **'at least you did. I got myself mixed up with myself in a corner.'** The idea of Sam violently fighting with himself and then his endearing honesty about this provides the reader with some light hearted moments. Yet any comic relief is undercut by the actions of the twins. Golding shows the descent into violence even in the twins, whose cheerful, amiable personalities have been a constant throughout the novel. Near the end, the twins are **'locked in an embrace, fighting each other'** but this is not entertaining; it is horrific and indicative of the terrible savagery that the boys have unleashed in themselves. If Sam and Eric, the identical twins, are violent to one another, there is little hope that the other boys will be able to resist their brutal urges. Their fighting is not funny; it is tragic. Golding possibly uses Lord of the Flies to present a religious *allegory* with the boys in a Garden of Eden and then falling into sin. The two fighting brothers are representative of Cain and Abel from the Bible and remind us of how we are doomed to violence.

☑ Finish with an overview

Sam and Eric's journey through the novel represents the experience of the ordinary boy. Their cheerful happiness is eroded by fear and violence until they betray Ralph's hiding place under torture. Yet they are, like all of us, also capable of savagery and Golding uses the twins to illustrate how we all suffer from **'mankind's essential illness'** and that the consequences of giving in to this illness are truly terrible.

7 Good/Evil or Human Nature

Exploration of a Theme

Golding used 'Lord of the Flies' to explore his belief that all humans have a capacity for evil. He believed that, if the restraints of society were stripped away then, in the end, savagery would win over civilisation and a desire to be good.

> 'We're not savages. We're English and the English are the best at everything'

THE BRITISH EMPIRE in 1920

• Jack agrees with Ralph that there should be rules on the island.

• His emphatic **declarative statements** reveal a nationalistic confidence. He is proud of his English heritage that marks him as superior to **'savages'**. He sees himself as civilised and morally sound and that, by being English, he is far removed from any primitive urges or savage instincts. He believes that his nationality and upbringing ensure that he will be a force for the good.

Context: Jack's comment shows a patriotic pride that echoes back to colonial thinking when the British Empire stretched across the world and national confidence in the superiority of English society was entrenched. Golding undermines any sense of English superiority; after all, immediately after Jack's confident statement, his fire soon spreads out of control and kills the little boy with the birthmark. It seems that simply being English will not be enough hold back evil and keep the boys good.

> **'Roger's arm was conditioned by a civilisation that knew nothing of him and was in ruins'**

• Roger throws stones at the littluns but holds back from hurting them with a direct aim. His arm is **'conditioned'** not to hurt the littluns, implying that goodness, kindness and a desire to protect is not part of our human nature. These elements are taught to us by society and **'civilisation'**. It is violence that comes naturally to us.

• Yet violence also comes to civilisation; the world of adults and civilised behaviour is **'in ruins'**, destroyed by bombs.

• *Structurally*, this episode is important as Roger moves closer to hurting the other children. The reader sees how civilisation **'knew nothing of him'** and so Roger will soon realise this and be free of its rules and restrictions that are the only thing that prevents him from violence and evil.

Context: The end of World War Two was marked by the dropping of atomic bombs on Japan. The fear of nuclear war was a constant threat in the post-war world; in the novel, Golding uses this contemporary idea of a world caught up in an atomic war as a background to the plot.

> **'the mask was a thing of its own, behind which Jack hid, liberated from shame and self-consciousness'**

• Jack paints his face in coloured mud, creating a mask. The mask allows Jack to explore his dark instincts which lead to violence. The mask ensures that Jack is **'liberated'**, free from the society's expectations of good behaviour.

• Alternatively, the mask could reflect how civilisation itself is just a mask, covering our innate sense of evil. Once the mask of civilisation is taken off, human nature is seen to be violent and evil. Jack can now be himself and indulge in all his previously hidden desires to hurt.

> **'the rules are the only thing we've got!'**

- Ralph is aware of the importance of rules as the foundation of their society and the last barrier against raw human nature and its desire for evil.

- The *exclamatory sentence* captures his passion; Ralph knows that the existence of their fragile society hangs on a knife edge and he is desperate to keep the community functioning.

- Ralph clings to the remnants of society and civilisation as he remembers it; he resists the dark side of his human nature.

Context: Golding uses Ralph and Jack to represent two schools of thought on how society should be run: Ralph represents democracy while Jack is moving towards a dictatorship. In this, Golding draws parallels with the recent World War 2, often viewed as a struggle between opposing ideologies.

Grade 9 Exploration:
Look at the theme in a different way

Does Golding leave us with any hope for humankind to conquer our natural desire for savagery?

Yes: Almost the last words of the novel are **'Ralph wept for the end of innocence, the darkness of man's heart, and the fall through the air of the true, wise friend called Piggy'**. There is a huge *pathos* in Ralph's tears as he sees how he has lost his childhood and witnessed unspeakable acts yet his recognition of the **'darkness of man's heart'** gives the reader hope that we can learn from our experiences and so build up a defence against our instincts towards savagery. The noble language of **'true, wise friend'** elevates and honours Piggy; in this, there is hope for the future.

No: Ralph is saved by a naval officer who is equipped with **'white drill, epaulettes, a revolver'**. It is only organised violence which saves Ralph from death, and the boys will be returning to a world rocked by an atomic bomb. It seems that humankind is doomed to repeat vicious cycles of savagery, reverting to the basest of human nature and learning nothing.

William Golding wrote in an essay that the boys in the novel are 'suffering from the terrible disease of being human'. He uses the novel to illustrate that violence and evil are part of our human condition.

Jack believes that his nationality and upbringing ensure that he will be a force for the good.

Jack's mask ensures that he is **'liberated'**, free from the society's expectations of good behaviour.

'We're not savages'

'the mask was a thing of its own, behind which Jack hid, liberated from shame '

The boys begin the story holding onto civilisation.

The boys find that they are drawn to evil.

Good/Evil or Human Nature

Some characters resist evil.

Does Golding leave us with any hope for humankind to conquer our natural desire for savagery?

'the rules are the only thing we've got!'

Yes: Ralph's tears at the end leaves us with hope that we can learn from our experiences and so build up a defence against our instincts towards savagery.

Ralph clings to the remnants of society and civilisation as he remembers it; he resists the dark side of his human nature.

No: It is only organised violence which saves Ralph from death, and the boys will be returning to a world rocked by an atomic bomb.

Sample GCSE Exam Question

Q: How does Golding use his novel to explore ideas about good and evil?

 # Sample GCSE Answer

☑ Introduction: start with an overview

Golding used 'Lord of the Flies' to explore his belief that all humans have a capacity for evil. He believed that the restraints of society force us to behave in a morally good way but, if these restraints are stripped away then, in the end, savagery will win over civilisation and humans will commit evil acts. The characters and the plot of the novel are carefully constructed to explore these ideas of good and evil.

☑ Make the point that the novel begins with the characters sticking to the moral frameworks that they are familiar with

At the start of the novel, the boys hold onto the moral frameworks that they have been brought up with and Jack agrees with Ralph that there should be rules on the island, saying **'we're not savages. We're English and the English are the best at everything'**. His emphatic *declarative statements* reflect a nationalistic confidence and that he is proud of his English heritage that marks him as superior to **'savages'**. He sees himself as civilised and morally sound and that, by being English, he is far removed from any primitive urges or savage instincts. Jack's comment reveals a patriotic pride that echoes back to colonial thinking when the British Empire stretched across the world and national confidence in the superiority of English society was entrenched. Golding undermines any sense of English superiority; after all, immediately after Jack's confident **statement**, his fire soon spreads out of control and kills the little boy with the birthmark. It seems that simply being English will not be enough hold back evil and keep the boys good.

☑ Move to the point that the characters are drawn to evil

Certainly, as the boys are stranded for an extended period of time, they begin to reject good and to embrace evil. Roger throws stones at the littluns but holds back from hurting them with a direct aim: **'Roger's arm was conditioned by a civilisation that knew nothing of him and was in ruins'**. Roger's arm is **'conditioned'** not to hurt the littluns, implying that kindness and a desire to protect is not part of our human nature. These elements are taught to us by society and **'civilisation'**. It is violence that comes naturally to us, not kindness and compassion. Interestingly, violence also comes to civilisation; the world of adults and civilised behaviour was **'in ruins'**, destroyed by an atomic bomb. *Structurally*, this episode is important as Roger moves closer to hurting the other children. The reader sees how civilisation **'knew nothing of him'** and so Roger will soon realise this and be free of its rules and restrictions. His innate desire to hurt will be let loose. The end of World War Two was marked by the dropping of atomic bombs on Japan and the possibility of nuclear war remained a threat in the post-war world; in the novel, Golding taps into this idea of a world caught up in an atomic war and which **'knew nothing'** of the stranded children as a background to the plot. It is not just Roger who relishes the opportunity to turn to evil; Golding constructs the character of Jack to show how he shifts from someone who prides himself on being morally sound and **'English'** to someone

48   SAMPLE GCSE ANSWER   LORD OF THE FLIES

who paints his face in coloured mud, creating the effect of a mask: **'the mask was a thing of its own, behind which Jack hid, liberated from shame and self-consciousness'**. The mask allows Jack to explore his dark instincts which lead him to violence. Interestingly, the mask ensures that Jack is **'liberated'**, showing how he is free from the restraints that society places on behaviour and can delve into his evil side.

☑ Move to the point that some characters try to resist evil

The island *setting* allows the boys to explore their savage instincts but there are some characters who try to resist evil. Ralph is aware of the importance of rules as the foundation of their society and the last barrier against raw human nature as he cries out to Jack **'the rules are the only thing we've got!'** The *exclamatory sentence* captures his passion; Ralph knows that the existence of their fragile society hangs on a knife edge and he is desperate to keep the community functioning. He clings to the remnants of society and civilisation as he remembers them, resisting the dark side of his human nature.

☑ Explore whether good or evil wins at the end of the novel

By the end of the novel, it seems that Golding does leave us with some hope for humankind, and that it is possible to conquer our human nature and our desire for savagery and evil. Almost the last words of the novel are **'Ralph wept for the end of innocence, the darkness of man's heart, and the fall through the air of the true, wise friend called Piggy'**. There is huge *pathos* in Ralph's tears as he sees how he has lost his childhood and witnessed unspeakable acts yet his recognition of the **'darkness of man's heart'** gives the reader hope that we can learn from our experiences and so build up a defence against the instincts towards savagery. The noble language of **'true, wise friend'** elevates and honours Piggy; in this, there is hope for the future. In this sense, the novel is a *bildungsroman*, a genre where the central character learns maturity. Ralph has learnt about the dark side of human nature and cannot forget this, returning to 'civilisation' a changed character. The reader is reassured that he will use these lessons to fight for good, not evil. Yet this is only one reading of the ending, and it is possible to see the novel's final message as an overwhelmingly pessimistic one. Ralph is saved by a naval officer who is equipped with **'white drill, epaulettes, a revolver'**. It is only organised violence which saves Ralph from death, and they will be returning to a world rocked by an atomic bomb. It seems that humankind is doomed to repeat vicious cycles of savagery, reverting to the basest of human nature and learning nothing. William Golding wrote in an essay that the boys in the novel are 'suffering from the terrible disease of being human' and he subverts the genre of children's adventure books such as 'Coral Island' and 'Swallows & Amazons'. In these stories, the children live outside the world of grown-ups and enjoy great camaraderie and adventure throughout the novels until they are reunited with the adult world at the end. Yet Golding twists this genre to show the bleak savagery at the heart of us all as the boys on the island violently turn on each other.

☑ Finish with an overview

In the pessimistic world of 'Lord of the Flies', Golding presents boys whose inner savagery is unleashed with dreadful consequences. He uses his dystopian novel to explore how violence and evil are part of our human condition and that, while we might resist our dark desires, they are so strong that, given the right circumstances, that they will dominate us.

8 Setting
Exploration of a Theme

The island is an ambiguous place. It is a place of great natural beauty with glorious features that the boys rejoice in yet it is also full of dangers which intimidate and threaten them.

'vision of red and yellow....witch-like cry'

- A beautiful bird makes a sound which is a **'witch-like cry'**.

- The island is a place of great beauty; the bird is described as a **'vision of red and yellow'**. The colour *adjectives* give a sense of glorious brightness and the word **'vision'** suggests that the bird is a thing of wonder.

- Yet the bird also has a **'witch-like cry'**. The *simile* suggests that the bird is evil with unpleasant intentions, perhaps *foreshadowing* the horrors that the boys will experience.

- The island is therefore established as a place of ambiguity and this is unsettling for the boys and for the readers.

'The creepers were as thick as their thighs... 'This is real exploring''

- Ralph, Simon and Jack excitedly investigate the island on their first day, finding thick creepers that need to crawled through.

- The island at first seems to offer a genuine adventure to the boys. Their exploration is full of eager discovery and the diverse island offers plenty of opportunity for exploits.
thing that prevents him from violence and evil.

Context: At first, 'Lord of the Flies' seems to fit the genre of castaway novels such as 'Coral Island' and 'Swallows and Amazons' with the boys cheerfully ranging across the island. Yet Golding subverts the genre; by the time that Simon is hacked to death, the boys have left behind any jolly adventuring and show they are more than capable of bloody murder.

'candle-like buds'

- Simon withdraws into the forest to be alone with nature.

- The **setting** is used to reflect characters. Simon finds a peaceful, beautiful place where it is quiet and serene; the **imagery** of the buds being **'candle-like'** helps create an atmosphere of a church or a temple.

- Simon retreats from the boys' company to be at one with nature, reflecting his spiritual nature. He has a perception and thoughtfulness that set him out as an outsider.thing that prevents him from violence and evil.

Context: Golding possibly uses Lord of the Flies to present a religious **allegory** with the boys in a Garden of Eden and then falling into sin. Simon's withdrawal from society and his links with **'candle-like buds'** establish him as the Christ figure in this **allegory**.

'The dark sky was shattered by a blue white scar'

- Simon is killed in the middle of a storm.

- **Setting** is used to create **dramatic tension**. Golding uses the weather to reveal the violent horror of Simon's death. Simon is seen as having an affinity with nature so this disruption of nature in the use of a storm reflects the brutality of his death. Tension is heightened with the terrible storm.

'rotten place' 'wizard fort'

• When they find Castle Rock, Ralph calls it a **'rotten place'** while Jack sees it as a **'wizard fort'**.

• **Setting** reflects ideas in the novel; here, the idea of good and evil. Ralph is repelled by Castle Rock and its gloomy, oppressive atmosphere but Jack immediately sees it as a place of military value.

Context: Golding uses Jack and Ralph to represent two opposing ideologies: Jack represents an authoritarian leader, one who uses physical force to control his followers. Jack is perhaps used as an allegory of Adolf Hitler. Ralph represents the forces of democracy, struggling to protect the littleuns and harmoniously manage the community. The boys' different reactions to the fort reflect these different ideas.

Grade 9 Exploration:
Look at the theme in a different way

Does the island force out the evil in the boys?

Yes: The island is full of wildlife such as the pigs that the boys have to hunt in order to obtain all their nutritional needs. This forces them to open up to their suppressed bloodlust which then spirals out of control. The boys are also completely surrounded by the vicious, uncaring elements of the island- the burning sun, the sudden storms- and eventually these overwhelm the young boys. The island is a barrier to the boys and their attempts to remain civilised; it is questionable, for example, whether Ralph and Piggy would have joined in the murder of Simon without the trigger of the unsettling, brutal storm which created such a dark, confusing atmosphere. The setting is a powerful catalyst in pushing the boys towards their downhill spiral into savagery.

No: The island merely provides the backdrop for the boys' descent into evil. It is Simon who realises that the evil is an intrinsic part of human nature as the Lord of the Flies tells him that **'I'm part of you. Close, close, close!'** There is a sense of *foreshadowing* in the *repetition* of the words **'close'**; each time, the Lord of the Flies reminds Simon just how fragile the veneer of civilisation is. Simon has the perception to see that the Beast is inside us all, and to recognise the darkness of man's heart. He knows that setting does not create evil; evil is already inside us.

Golding fought in World War Two and saw even the best of men give in to savagery and brutality. Golding view the violence and cruelty in us as the 'terrible disease' of being human; he saw evil as an internal force, not one created by environment.

Colour **adjectives** establish the bird's beauty but the **simile** suggests evil and danger.

Simon finds a peaceful place to be alone. The **imagery** of the buds being **'candle-like'** creates an atmosphere of a church or a temple, mirroring his spiritual personality.

'vision of red and yellow... witch-like cry'

'candle-like buds'

The island setting is exotic but dangerous.

Setting helps to define the characters.

Setting

Setting reflects themes.

Does the island force out the evil in the boys?

'rotten place' 'wizard fort'

Yes: The island's wildife allows for hunting which forces the boys to open up to their suppressed bloodlust which then spirals out of control.

The boys' reactions to Castle Rock reflects ideas of good and evil. Ralph is repelled by Castle Rock's gloomy atmosphere but Jack sees it as a place of military value.

No: The island merely provides the backdrop for the boys' descent into evil. Golding saw evil as an internal force, not one created by environment.

Sample GCSE Exam Question

Q: What is the significance of setting in 'Lord of the Flies'?

 # Sample GCSE Answer

✓ Start with an overview about the *setting* of the novel

The island in 'Lord of the Flies' is an ambiguous place. It is a place of great natural beauty with glorious features that the boys rejoice in yet it is also full of dangers which intimidate and threaten them. Golding uses the *setting* to explore themes and characters and also to drive the plot towards its painful, terrifying ending.

✓ Make the point that the island is a place of both excitement and danger

The island *setting* allows Golding to create an environment which is both exciting and dangerous. In the opening pages, a bird is described as a **'vision of red and yellow'** with a **'witch-like cry'**. The reader and the stranded boys view the island as a place of great beauty; the bird is described as a **'vision of red and yellow'** and the colour *adjectives* give a sense of glorious brightness while the word **'vision'** shows that the bird is a thing of wonder. Yet the bird also has a **'witch-like cry'**. The *simile* suggests that the bird is evil with unpleasant intentions, perhaps *foreshadowing* the horrors that the boys will experience. The island is therefore established as a place of ambiguity and this is unsettling for the boys and for the readers. Yet the wild *setting* also allows the boys freedom to have a true adventure. Ralph, Simon and Jack excitedly investigate the island on their first day, finding creepers **'as thick as their thighs'** so that Jack exclaims that **'this is real exploring'** and the island at first seems to offer a genuine adventure to the boys. Their exploration is full of eager discovery and the diverse island offers plenty of opportunity for exploits. At the start of the novel, 'Lord of the Flies' seems to fit the genre of castaway novels such as 'Coral Island' and 'Swallows and Amazons' with the boys cheerfully ranging across the island. Yet Golding subverts the genre; by the time Simon is hacked to death, the boys have left behind any jolly adventuring and show they are more than capable of bloody murder.

✓ Move to the point that the *setting* helps to establish characters

The *setting* is not just a backdrop for the action of the novel; Golding also uses the *setting* to help establish the characters. An example of this is with Simon, who withdraws into the forest to be alone with nature and sits alone with the **'candle-like buds'**. This natural clearing is a peaceful, beautiful place where it is quiet and serene; the *imagery* of the buds being **'candle-like'** helps create an atmosphere of a church or a temple. Simon retreats from the boys' company to be at one with nature, reflecting his spiritual nature. He has a perception and thoughtfulness that set him out as an outsider. Golding possibly uses Lord of the Flies to present a religious *allegory* with the boys in a Garden of Eden and then falling into sin. Simon's withdrawal from society and his links with **'candle-like buds'** establish him as the Christ figure in this *allegory*. The *setting* therefore helps illustrate and define the characters.

☑ Examine how Golding uses the *setting* to explore themes

The *setting* also works to illustrate the themes in the novel. When the boys find Castle Rock, Ralph calls it a **'rotten place'** while Jack sees it as a **'wizard fort'**. Their reactions to the new place reflect ideas about good and evil. Ralph is repelled by Castle Rock and its gloomy, oppressive atmosphere but Jack immediately sees it as a place of great military value. Golding uses Jack and Ralph to represent two opposing ideologies: Jack represents an authoritarian leader, one who uses physical force to control his followers. Jack is perhaps used as an *allegory* of Adolf Hitler. Ralph represents the forces of democracy and one who struggles to protect the littleuns and seek good. The boys' different reactions to the fort reflect these different ideas as Jack sees it as a stronghold to consolidate his power and Ralph is uneasy about the foreboding atmosphere.

☑ Explore how far the *setting* works as an active force in the boys' move towards

Setting is used by Golding to explore his central theme: that of the darkness of human nature. The island is a place which allows the boys to be free from the constraints of civilisation and explore their inner savagery. Arguably, the island forces out the evil in the boys. The island is full of wildlife such as the pigs that the boys have to hunt in order to obtain all their nutritional needs. This act of hunting forces them to open up to their bloodlust which then spirals out of control. The boys are also completely surrounded by the vicious, uncaring elements of the island, such as the burning sun and the sudden storms, and eventually these overwhelm the young boys. The island is impervious to the boys and their attempts to remain civilised; it is questionable, for example, whether Ralph and Piggy would have joined in the murder of Simon without the catalyst of the unsettling, brutal storm which created such a dark, confusing atmosphere. Yet this is only one view; another is that the island merely provides the backdrop for the boys' descent into evil. Evil is within us all, as Simon understands when he hears the Lord of the Flies tell him just how fragile the human conscience is and just how fragile the veneer of civilisation is, that **'I'm part of you. Close, close, close!'** The island *setting* does not force the boys into evil; it is simply the framework for the action. Golding fought in World War Two and saw even the best of men give in to savagery and brutality. Golding regarded the violence and cruelty in us as the 'terrible disease' of being human; he saw evil as an internal force, not one created by environment.

☑ Finish with an overview

In the pessimistic world of 'Lord of the Flies', Golding creates an island *setting* which works effectively as an exotic, mysterious backdrop to the action. Yet the *setting* also successfully works to help define the characters, to heighten tension and to illustrate Golding's central theme: that, while we might resist our dark desire for violence, it is so strong that, given the right circumstances, it will dominate us.

9 Friendship
Exploration of a Theme

In the novel, a group of boys are thrown together in an unusual situation on a deserted island. They are fairly similar in age and from reasonably similar backgrounds which ensures that friendships are easily formed. Yet, even at the start, there are divisions in the friendships as humankind's base desire for power exerts itself.

'strange invisible light of friendship, adventure and content'

• Jack and Ralph sit in front of the fire they have jointly made, pleased with their work and enjoying each other's company.

• Golding celebrates the collaborative efforts that the boys have made through using a **metaphor** of light. The **list** of **nouns** captures the optimism that the boys still have in the early days on the island.

• There is perhaps **foreshadowing** in the **adjective 'strange'** which suggests that this bond of friendship is unusual or hard to define. Certainly, the friendships are soon torn apart as time wears on and attempts to conform to civilisation on the island break down.

Context: Golding subverts the genre of children's adventure books such as 'Coral Island' and 'Swallows and Amazons'. In these stories, the children live outside the world of grown-ups and enjoy great camaraderie and adventure throughout the novels until they are reunited with the adult world at the end. Yet Golding twists this genre to show the bleak savagery at the heart of us all as the boys on the island violently turn on each other, destroying any semblance of friendship.

"Better Piggy than Fatty,' he said.'	• Ralph betrays his new friend Piggy by telling the boys of the nickname that Piaggy is ashamed of. • Friendships should be based on trust and Ralph betrays this trust. Arguably, he does this for Piggy's good in order to deflect a worse nickname. Yet it seems to Piggy that Ralph has betrayed him at the first opportunity.	**Context:** Golding was a school teacher and saw first-hand the alliances and betrayals of the school boys that he taught.

'we want meat' 'we need shelters'	• Jack and Ralph's friendship is tested by their different priorities: Jack's priority is to indulge in the excitement of hunting while Ralph is concerned with providing shelters. • The opposition is clear in the similar **sentence structure** which reflects the conflict that is testing their friendship. The shift in **verbs** from **'want'** to **'need'** shows the friendship is in conflict as Jack wishes to indulge his desires and Ralph is putting his own desires to one side to provide for the community.	**Context:** Golding uses Ralph and Jack to represent two opposing ideologies: Ralph represents a paternalistic democracy where the needs of the weak are looked after while Jack is moving towards a dictatorship based on brutal violence. In this, Golding draws parallels with the recent World War Two, often viewed as a struggle between opposing ideologies. In this struggle, friendships soon become impossible.

'link… snapped and fastened elsewhere'

• After the confrontation over the dead fire and the failed attempt to be rescued, Jack and Ralph's friendship changes.

• The **metaphor** of friendship being a chain which holds people together is used to show how Ralph ceases to value his relationship with Jack.

• Ralph grows closer to Piggy who **'could think'**. Ralph looks beyond the outward appearance of the chubby, socially awkward Piggy and starts to value him.

'only just avoiding pushing him with his shoulder'

• Roger takes over the torture of Sam and Eric, pushing past Jack and **'only just avoiding pushing him with his shoulder'**.

• Roger and Jack bond because they share the same desire to hunt and to hurt. Here, we see the facade of friendship stripped away as Roger takes control in a barely veiled challenge. Desire for power and violence has replaced friendships on the island.

Grade 9 Exploration:
Look at the theme in a different way

Are the friendships that are formed on the island genuine?

Yes: Ralph is the central figure in the novel and we see most events through his eyes as the novel follows his story, starting and ending with his experiences. At the end, **'Ralph wept for... the fall through the air of the true, wise friend called Piggy'**. There is huge *pathos* in Ralph's tears as he mourns the loss of Piggy and understands Piggy's loyalty and intelligence. In this sense, the reader sees how genuine this friendship was and how Ralph has learnt valuable lessons about what friendship means.

In this sense, the novel is a *bildungsroman*, a genre where the central character learns maturity. Ralph has learnt about the dark side of human nature and cannot forget this, returning to civilisation a changed character and one who has learnt about real friendship.

No: The friendships in the novel are not genuine: for example, Ralph and Piggy's companionship is based on necessity and their joint desire to be rescued. Similarly, Jack and Roger's alliance is not founded on great liking or trust but on a deep base desire to let unleash their violent urges. There seems little doubt that, if the naval officers had not arrived, then all of the boys would have eventually turned on each other in a survival of the fittest with not even a cursory pretence at friendship.

William Golding believed that human nature is evil and that the boys are suffering from the 'terrible disease of being human'. As the boys move further away from civilisation and its restraints, they start to succumb to this disease. Friendship is one of the casualties of the descent into savagery; in a survival of the fittest, there is no room for the civilised bonds of friendship.

The *adjectives* capture how the boys cheefully bond with one another, caught up in the excitement and novelty of their situation.

Jack and Ralph's friendship is tested by their different priorities. Jack's priority is to indulge in the excitement of hunting while Ralph is concerned with providing shelters.

'happy, heaving pile'

'we want meat' 'we need shelters'

The boys form bonds of friendship at the start.

Friendships begin to fracture.

Friendship

Friendships are destroyed by individual desires for power and violence.

Are any of the friendships on the island genuine?

'only just avoiding pushing him with his shoulder'

Yes: Ralph weeps at the end for **'the true, wise friend called Piggy'**. He has learnt the value of genuine friendship based on loyalty.

Roger and Jack's bond is based on mutual desires rather than friendship and, by the end, this bond is really fragile.

No: The friendships are based on necessity and falsehoods. They fall apart as the boys descend into savagery.

Sample GCSE Exam Question

Q: 'Ralph and Jack smiled at each other with shy liking.' Explore the theme of friendship in 'Lord of the Flies'.

Sample GCSE Answer

☑ Start with an overview on the theme of friendship

In Golding's dystopian novel 'Lord of the Flies,' a group of boys are thrown together in an unusual situation on a deserted island. They are fairly similar in age and from reasonably similar backgrounds which ensures that friendships are easily formed. Yet, even at the start, there are divisions in the friendships as humankind's base desire for power exerts itself.

☑ Make the point that the novel starts with the boys forming bonds of friendship

 The novel opens with the boys from the crashed aeroplane meeting together and forming bonds of friendship. There is a spirit of excitement in the novelty of their situation and this helps cement early friendships. At the end of the first day, Jack and Ralph sit in front of the fire they have jointly made, enjoying each other's company in a **'strange invisible light of friendship, adventure and content'**. Golding celebrates the collaborative efforts that the boys have made through using a *metaphor* of light. The *list* of *nouns* captures the optimism that the boys still have in the early days on the island. There is perhaps *foreshadowing* in the *adjective* **'strange'** which suggests that this bond of friendship is unusual. Certainly, the friendships are soon torn apart as time wears on and attempts to conform to civilisation on the island break down. Golding subverts the genre of children's adventure books such as 'Coral Island' and 'Swallows and Amazons'. In these stories, the children live outside the world of grown-ups and enjoy great camaraderie throughout the novels until they are reunited with the adult world at the end. Yet Golding twists this genre to show the savagery at the heart of us all as the boys on the island violently turn on each other, destroying any semblance of friendship.

☑ Move to the point that the friendships are tested

Certainly, these friendships show tension even at the beginning. Piggy trusts Ralph to not tell the other boys of the nickname that he is ashamed of but Ralph lets Piggy down only minutes after Piggy's sharing of his secret. Friendships should be based on trust and Ralph betrays this trust. Golding was a school teacher and saw first-hand the alliances and betrayals of the school boys that he taught. Deeper divisions in the friendship groups quickly occur; the friendship of Jack and Ralph is tested by their different priorities and comes to a head with Jack stating **'we want meat'** and Ralph arguing that the group's energy should be redirected as **'we need shelters'**. Jack's priority is to indulge in the excitement of hunting while Ralph is concerned with providing safety for the community. The opposition is clear in the similar *sentence structure* which reflects the conflict that is testing their friendship. The shift in *verbs* from **'want'** to **'need'** illustrates that the friendship is in conflict as Jack wishes to indulge his desires and Ralph is putting his own desires to one side to provide for the community. Golding uses Ralph and Jack to represent two opposing ideologies: Ralph represents a paternalistic democracy where the needs of the weak are looked after while Jack is moving towards a dictatorship based on brutal violence. In this, Golding draws parallels with the recent World War Two, often viewed as a struggle between opposing ideologies. In this struggle, friendships soon become impossible.

☑ Make the point that real friendship is discovered in unlikely places

The friendship between Jack and Ralph is destroyed after the confrontation over the dead fire and the failed attempt to be rescued. Friendship is described as a **'link'** which **'snapped and fastened elsewhere'**. This *metaphor* of friendship being a chain which holds people together is used to show how Ralph ceases to value his relationship with Jack. Ralph grows closer to Piggy who **'could think'**. Ralph looks beyond the outward appearance of the chubby, socially awkward Piggy and starts to value him. Golding offers the reader a positive view of friendships through this relationship; Ralph is the central figure in the novel and we see most events through his eyes as the novel follows his story, starting and ending with his experiences. At the end, **'Ralph wept for... the fall through the air of the true, wise friend called Piggy'**. There is huge *pathos* in Ralph's tears as he mourns the loss of Piggy and understands Piggy's loyalty and intelligence. In this sense, the reader sees how genuine this friendship was and how Ralph has learnt valuable lessons about what friendship means. The novel is a ***bildungsroman***, a genre where the central character learns maturity. Ralph has learnt about the dark side of human nature and cannot forget this, returning to civilisation a changed character and one who has learnt about real friendship.

☑ Examine whether we are left with any positive views of friendship

However, there is an argument that Golding does not present any positive view of friendships in the novel. Ralph and Piggy's friendship is based on necessity and ends with Piggy's murder and, elsewhere in the novel, friendships are undermined by falsehoods and a desire for power; an example of this is Roger and Jack, who bond because they share the same desire to hunt and to hurt. This is not a solid friendship and, towards the end, Roger takes over the torture of Sam and Eric, pushing past Jack and **'only just avoiding pushing him with his shoulder'**. Here, we see the facade of friendship stripped away as Roger takes control in a barely veiled challenge. Desire for power and violence has replaced friendships on the island. There seems little doubt that, if the naval officers had not arrived, then all of the boys would have eventually turned on each other in a survival of the fittest with not even a cursory pretence at friendship. William Golding believed that human nature is evil and that the boys are suffering from the 'terrible disease of being human'. As the boys move further away from civilisation and its restraints, they start to succumb to this disease. Friendship is one of the casualties of the descent into savagery; in a survival of the fittest, there is no room for the civilised bonds of friendship.

☑ Finish with an overview

Golding presents a bleak view of humankind's capacity for genuine friendship as the desire for power and the love and fear of violent defines relationships. Yet perhaps the reader can take comfort from the doomed but genuine friendship between Piggy and Ralph; certainly, their friendship is one that the reader remembers.

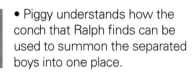10 Authority & Power
Exploration of a Theme

Golding explores how the desire for power destroys the boys' fragile community and leads to acts of unspeakable violence.

'we can use this to call a meeting'

• Piggy understands how the conch that Ralph finds can be used to summon the separated boys into one place.

• Golding uses the conch as a **symbol** of democracy in the novel. In the beginning, the boys emulate the society that they grew up in by choosing to organise their community through a democratic election and using the conch to allow all to have free speech.

• Yet, although Piggy knows what to do with the conch, he does not take the conch from Ralph. Piggy is aware that he will be seen as inferior to the tall, charismatic Ralph. Authority is naturally given to those who are physically superior.

'true leadership'

• Golding describes Ralph as having **'true leadership'**.

• He shows good instincts as a leader, making sensible decisions about shelters and latrines.

Context: Ralph represents civilised society and the paternalistic aspects of government, trying to make sure the community stays healthy and safe.

> 'the rules are the only thing we've got!'
>
> 'bollocks to the rules! We're strong- we hunt!'

- Ralph is aware of the importance of rules as the foundation of their society but Jack dismisses these rules and the power of the conch.

- Jack's use of the swear word **'bollocks'** shows just how much contempt he has for the rules of the community. At this point, Jack is realising that he can defy any regulations and follow his urges without any sanctions.

- These urges are clear in the short, emphatic *clauses* **'we're strong!- we hunt!'** which captures his desire for violence and shows where he places value. His values are not on rules and rational thought but on physical strength and blood lust, and the *exclamation marks* reflect his passion.

Context: Using Freudian analysis, Jack represents the 'id', the side of our personalities which seeks to fulfill our own desires regardless of society's rules.

> 'The chief was sitting there, naked to the waist....he pointed at this savage and that with his spear'

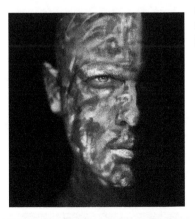

- Towards the end, Jack is in total control of his hunters.

- He is so far removed from the young chorister who arrived on the island that he has lost the name that links him to civilisation; instead of Jack, he is referred to as **'the chief'**.

- His rule and power is based on violence; the way that he uses his spear to point at his followers reflects this.

Context: Writing in the 1950s, Golding uses Jack and Ralph to represent two opposing ideologies: Jack represents an authoritarian leader. The recent World War Two was often seen as a struggle between democracy and dictatorship. Jack is perhaps used as an *allegory* of Adolf Hitler; certainly, he is a dictator, allowing his followers no freedom of action or freedom of speech.

| 'exploded into a thousand white fragments' | • Piggy is killed as he holds the conch which **'exploded into a thousand white fragments'**. | **Context:** Golding fought in World War Two and saw how violence and brutality consumed men. With the death of Piggy and the destruction of the conch, we see how violence overthrows the rule of law and there is no authority that will stop the boys exploring their inner savagery. |

• Piggy respects the values of free speech and rational thought right until the end. Yet this does not save him. With Piggy's death, the conch is shattered, *symbolising* the loss of order on the island. Violence is now the only power on the island.

Grade 9 Exploration:
Look at the theme in a different way

Does Golding leave us any hope that we can live in a way where desire for power is moderated and authority figures are fair?

Yes: There is hope in the figure of Simon who takes fruit from the trees to give to the littleuns, **'pull(ing) off the choicest'** fruit for them. Simon's innate kindness and generosity is shown in his actions, taking the time to help feed the weaker littluns. His selflessness is evident in the *superlative adjective* **'choicest'**, demonstrating how he gives the best fruit to the others rather than keeping it for himself. Simon works to help the others, revealing a collaborative approach that Golding approved of.

In Freudian analysis, Simon represents the superego. This is the idea of idealistic moral values and Simon's behaviour reflects this.

No: Ralph is saved by a naval officer who is equipped with **'white drill, epaulettes, a revolver'**. The authority of the adult saves Ralph from death but the symbols of the officer's power are evident in his uniform and his revolver. Even the adults, who should be wise, live in a society where authority comes from physical strength and the threat of violence.

Golding was interested in ideas of power and explored these in his other novels; his next novel, 'The Inheritors', tells of a group of brutal homo sapiens (men) who use violence to destroy a Neanderthal tribe. Golding's works present a bleak view of humankind's desire for power over others and how we use violence to achieve this power.

The conch is a *symbol* of democracy . The boys organise their community through a democratic election and using the conch to allow free speech.

Jack's use of the swear word **'bollocks'** shows how much contempt he has for the rules. Jack realises that he can defy regulations and follow his urges without any sanctions.

'we can use this to call a meeting'

'bollocks to the rules! We're strong- we hunt!'

The boys begin their time on the island by establishing a democracy.

Democratic power is challenged.

Authority & Power

By the end, the only power on the island is through violence.

Does Golding leave us any hope that we can live in a way where desire for power is moderated and authority figures are fair?

'exploded into a thousand white fragments'

Yes: Golding uses Simon to show us how we can work to help the others in a collaborative way.

With the death of Piggy and the destruction of the conch, we see how violence overthrows the democracy.

No: Ralph is saved by a naval officer. Even the adults, who should be wise, live in a society where authority comes from physical strength and the threat of violence.

Q: 'You voted me for chief. Now you do what I say.'

How does Golding explore ideas of authority and power in the novel?

Sample GCSE Answer

☑ Start with an overview about the ideas of authority and power in the novel

In his dystopian novel 'Lord of the Flies', Golding explores how the desire for power destroys the boys' fragile community and leads to acts of unspeakable violence.

☑ Make the point that the novel begins with the boys holding onto the structure of civilised society

The novel opens with the stranded boys spread out on the deserted island. Ralph finds the conch which Piggy immediately sees can be used **'to call a meeting'**. While Ralph is transfixed by the conch's beauty, Piggy sees the practical use of the conch, understanding how the conch can be used to summon the separated boys into one place. His words are sensible and pragmatic, revealing that there is a need to gather the boys in one place to begin to organise themselves. Golding uses the conch as a *symbol* of democracy in the novel and, in the beginning, the boys emulate the society that they grew up in by choosing to organise their community through a democratic election and then using the conch to allow all to have free speech. Interestingly, though, although Piggy knows what to do with the conch, he does not take the conch from Ralph. Piggy is aware that he will be seen as inferior to the tall, charismatic Ralph and even in the first pages of the novel, authority is naturally given to those who are physically superior. However, Ralph's leadership is based on free speech and equality which bodes well for their future on the island. Indeed, Golding describes Ralph as having **'true leadership'** as Ralph shows good instincts, making sensible decisions about shelters and latrines. By doing this, Ralph represents civilised society and the paternalistic aspects of government, trying to make sure the community stays healthy and safe.

☑ Move to the point that the boys' democratic community soon begins to break down

As time passes, the democracy of the community begins to come under threat as the memory of civilised society fades and the boys realise there is little to stop them indulging in their dark desire for violence. Tensions arise between the boys; Ralph is aware of the importance of rules as the foundation of their society, crying **'the rules are the only thing we've got!'** but Jack dismisses these rules and the power of the conch, saying **'bollocks to the rules! We're strong- we hunt!'** Jack's use of the swear word **'bollocks'** shows just how much contempt he has for the rules of the community. At this point, Jack is realising that he can defy any regulations and strictures and follow his own urges without any sanctions. These urges are clear in the short, emphatic *clauses* **'we're strong!- we hunt!'** which captures his desire for violence and shows where he places value. His values are not on rules and rational thought but on physical strength and blood lust, and the *exclamation marks* reflect his forceful passion. Using Freudian analysis, Jack represents the 'id', the side of our personalities which seeks to fulfill our own desires regardless of society's rules. As the democratic community begins to crumble, Jack becomes aware how he can take power through violence to satisfy his own needs. This results in a split in the community and Jack taking his hunters to form a separate group.

☑ Make the point that that power passes entirely to those who rule through violence

Towards the end, Jack is in total control of his hunters: **'the chief was sitting there, naked to the waist… he pointed at this savage and that with his spear'**. He is so far removed from the young chorister who arrived on the island that he has lost the name that links him to civilisation; instead of Jack, he is referred to as **'the chief'**. His rule and power is based on violence; the way that he uses his spear to point at his followers reflects this. Golding uses Jack and Ralph to represent two opposing ideologies with Jack representing an authoritarian leader. World War Two was often seen as a struggle between democracy and dictatorship. Jack is perhaps used as an ***allegory*** of Adolf Hitler; certainly, he is a dictator, allowing his followers no freedom of action or freedom of speech. Jack's absolute authority on the island is cemented with the death of Piggy who is pushed from the rock, clutching the conch which **'exploded into a thousand white fragments'**. Piggy respects the values of free speech and rational thought right until the end. Yet this does not save him. With Piggy's death, the conch is shattered, ***symbolising*** the loss of order and reason on the island. The violence of Piggy's death is caught in the powerful ***verb* 'exploded'** and the utter destruction of the conch into a **'thousand white fragments'**. Violence now reigns on the island. Golding fought in World War Two and saw how violence and brutality consumed men. With the death of Piggy and the destruction of the conch, we see how violence overthrows the rule of law and there is no authority that will stop the boys exploring their inner savagery which Golding witnessed in his war years.

☑ Finish with exploring whether Golding leaves us any hope that we can live in a way where desire for power is moderated and authority figures are fair

'Lord of the Flies' leaves us wondering whether Golding leaves us any hope that we can live in a way where desire for power is moderated and authority figures are fair. There is perhaps hope in the figure of Simon who takes fruit from the trees to give to the littleuns, **'pull(ing) off the choicest'** fruit for them. Simon's innate kindness and generosity is shown in his actions, taking the time to help feed the weaker littluns. His selflessness is evident in the ***superlative adjective* 'choicest'**, demonstrating how he gives the best fruit to the others rather than keeping it for himself. Simon works to help the others, revealing a collaborative approach that Golding approved of. In Freudian analysis, Simon represents the superego. This is the idea of idealistic moral values and Simon's behaviour reflects this, suggesting that there is hope that the positive side of human nature can lead us to organise society in a fair, democratic way. Yet this is only one view, and the end of the novel presents a different view of how humans organise society. Ralph is rescued by a naval officer who is equipped with **'white drill, epaulettes, a revolver'**. The authority of the adult saves Ralph from death but the symbols of the officer's power are evident in his uniform and his revolver. Even the adults, who should be wise, live in a society where authority comes from physical strength and the threat of violence. Golding was interested in ideas of power and explored these in his other novels; his next novel, 'The Inheritors', tells of a group of brutal homo sapiens (men) who use violence to destroy a Neanderthal tribe. Golding's works present a bleak view of humankind's desire for power over others and and how we use violence to achieve this power.

☑ Finish with an overview

'Lord of the Flies' gives us a story of a group of boys who try to establish a democracy but fail. Human nature causes the pillars of democracy to crumble until the boys are savages, ruled entirely by primitive urges and the fear of violence. It leaves us with a pessimistic view of how humankind organises society and establishes power.

11 Religion
Exploration of a Theme

'Lord of the Flies' is not simply a gripping story of a group of schoolboys stranded on an island; it works on a deeper level by using religious references to explore the complex nature of humankind: our desire for savagery and our desire for spirituality.

'vision of red and yellow... witch-like cry' 	• A beautiful bird makes a sound which is a **'witch-like cry'**. • The island is a place of great beauty; the bird is described as a **'vision of red and yellow'**. The colour *adjectives* give a sense of glorious brightness and the word **'vision'** suggests that the bird is a thing of wonder. • Yet the bird also has a **'witch-like cry'**. The *simile* suggests that the bird is evil with unpleasant intentions, perhaps *foreshadowing* the horrors that the boys will experience. • The island is therefore established as a place of ambiguity and this is unsettling for the boys and for the readers.	**Context:** Golding possibly uses 'Lord of the Flies' to present a religious *allegory* with the boys beginning the novel in a wonderful Garden of Eden and then falling into sin and darkness. There is a sense that the island is a place of unspoilt beauty yet, just as the snake lived in the garden of Eden, there is evil on the island and the bird's cry reminds us of this.
'Piggy' 'Shut up, Fatty'... Laughter arose...'	• Piggy is bullied. • As laughter surrounds him, Piggy is immediately established as a victim, as someone who is physically weaker and therefore open to abuse. Piggy generates hate and contempt; he is a vent for the boys' instinctive dark urges to hurt and humiliate, and Jack leads the way in constantly bullying him.	**Context:** Golding lived through the of the horrific persecution that the Jewish people experienced in 1930s and 1940s Europe. Possibly, in an *allegorical* novel where Jack represents the dictator Hitler, Piggy represents the Jewish people. Golding illustrates how people are persecuted because of their religion, and how religion can generate terrible hostility.

'candle-like buds'

- Simon withdraws into the forest to be alone with nature.

- Simon finds a peaceful, beautiful place where it is quiet and serene; the *imagery* of the buds being **'candle-like'** helps create an atmosphere of a church.

- Simon retreats from the boys' company to be at one with nature, reflecting his spiritual nature. He has a perception and thoughtfulness that set him out as an outsider.

Context: The concept of the novel as a religious *allegory* is returned to as Golding places Simon as the Christ figure. Simon's withdrawal from society and his links with **'candle-like buds'** establishes Simon as a representation of Jesus Christ with links to stories in the New Testament of how Jesus would leave his companions for solitary prayer.

'Lord of the Flies'

- The pig's head on the stick is named the **'Lord of the Flies'**. This translates into 'Beelzebub' in Greek, which is a name for the devil.

- Golding seems to link the idea of evil with the devil. The boys give tributes such as the pig's head to the beast out of fear and reverence for the power that they think the beast holds. This pagan practice to avert supernatural evil is something the boys quickly turn to.

Context: Golding held religious beliefs but was not a member of an established church. He explores ideas about faith within the novel.

'I'm part of you. Close, close, close!'

- It is Simon who realises that the evil is an intrinsic part of human nature as he talks to the Lord of the Flies.

- There is a sense of *foreshadowing* in the *repetition* of the words **'close'**; each time, the Lord of the Flies reminds Simon just how fragile the veneer of civilisation is. Simon has the perception to see that the Beast is inside us all, and to recognise the darkness of man's heart.

Context: Golding fought in World War Two and saw even the best of men give in to savagery and brutality. Golding saw the violence and cruelty in us as the 'terrible disease' of being human; he saw evil as an internal force that is part of us. There is no external devil to be frightened of but we should be frightened of ourselves.

> **'Kill the beast! Cut his throat! Spill his blood!'**

- The boys kill Simon in a frenzy of blood-lust.

- There is a sacrificial element to Simon's death, again reflecting his association with Christ who was murdered by his own people.

- Simon's death marks a changing point in the novel. The boys' descent into savagery is now unstoppable; by killing Simon, who embodies goodness, they are now free to unleash the darkness within them.

- It seems that the positive element of religion is easy to destroy.

Grade 9 Exploration:
Look at the theme in a different way

Is 'Lord of the Flies' an anti-religious text?

Yes: Golding uses the novel to illustrate the dangers of religion which divides society and can be exploited to explore our savage urges. An example of this is just before Simon's death when Jack is elevated to god-like status; the hunters drag out a log where **'Jack, painted and garlanded, sat there like an idol'**. With this status of a deity to be worshipped, he is able to whip the boys into violence which ends in murder. Golding is possibly suggesting that humankind needs religion to justify our natural brutality.

No: Simon's goodness and inherent understanding reflects how religion draws us to spirituality and away from savagery. Simon takes fruit from the trees to give to the littluns; he **'pulled off the choicest'** fruit for them. Simon's innate kindness and generosity is shown in his actions, taking the time to help feed the weaker littluns. His selflessness is shown in the **superlative adjective 'choicest'**, demonstrating how he gives the best fruit to the others rather than keeping it for himself. As the Christ- figure, he brings understanding and perception and provides hope that religion can protect us from our brutal inner desires.

 # Essential Exam Tip

☑ Make sure your answer covers the whole novel. Don't make all your points about just the start or just the end. Show the examiner that you have a good knowledge of how the story develops and how the characters change

The island **setting** with its stunning wildlife represents the Garden of Eden. There is evil waiting there for the boys, as suggested by the bird's cry.

The pig's head is used in a pagan way as a sacrifice to some powerful supernatural force. 'Lord of the Flies' translates into Beelzebub, meaning 'devil'.

'vision of red and yellow'
'witch-like cry'

'Lord of the Flies'

The novel is a religious *allegory*.

Evil is linked to the devil.

Religion

Ideas of religious persecution are explored through Piggy, who perhaps is an *allegorical* figure for the Jewish race.

Is 'Lord of the Flies' an anti-religious text?

'Piggy' 'Shut up, Fatty' 'Laughter arose...'

Yes: Golding uses the novel to illustrate the dangers of religion which can be exploited to explore our savage urges. Jack takes on a god-like status as an **'idol'** and exploits this to whip the boys into violence.

Piggy's persecution could reflect the appalling experience of the European Jews in the1930s and 1940s. Religion can generate terrible hostility.

No: Simon's goodness and inherent understanding reflects how religion draws us to spirituality and away from savagery.

Sample GCSE Exam Question

Q: Explore how far 'Lord of the Flies' is a religious text.

 # Sample GCSE Answer

☑ Start with an overview about the ideas of religion in the novel

'Lord of the Flies' is not simply a gripping story of a group of schoolboys stranded on an island; it works on a deeper level by using religious references to explore the complex nature of humankind: our desire for savagery and our desire for spirituality.

☑ Make the point that Golding uses many religious references in the novel

Golding possibly uses 'Lord of the Flies' to present a religious *allegory* with the boys beginning the novel in a wonderful Garden of Eden and then falling into sin and darkness. The *setting* is reminiscent of the unspoilt Garden of Eden from the opening pages and Golding describes a bird as a **'vision of red and yellow'**. The colour *adjectives* give a sense of glorious brightness and the word **'vision'** suggests that the bird is a thing of wonder. Yet the bird also has a **'witch-like cry'**. The *simile* suggests that the bird is evil with unpleasant intentions, perhaps *foreshadowing* the horrors that the boys will experience. The island is therefore established as a place of ambiguity and this is unsettling for the boys and for the readers. There is a sense that the island is a place of unspoilt beauty yet, just as the snake lived in the garden of Eden, there is evil on the island and the bird's cry reminds us of this.

☑ Continue with the exploration of the novel as a religious *allegory*

The concept of the novel as a religious *allegory* is continually returned to; an example of this is Golding's presentation of Simon as a Christ figure. Simon withdraws into the forest to be alone with nature, finding a peaceful, beautiful place with **'candle-like buds'** where it is quiet and serene; the *imagery* of the buds being **'candle-like'** helps create an atmosphere of a church or a temple. His perception and spirituality sets him apart as an outsider and links to stories in the New Testament of how Jesus would leave his companions for solitary prayer. Simon also displays innate kindness and generosity when he **'pulled off the choicest'** fruit for the littleuns from the trees. His selflessness is shown in the *superlative adjective* **'choicest'**, demonstrating how he takes time to look after the weaker young boys and gives the best fruit to the others rather than keeping it for himself; this again connects him with the purity and selflessness of Christ. Simon's goodness and inherent understanding reflects how religion draws us to spirituality and away from savagery. As the Christ-figure, Simon brings understanding and perception and provides hope that religion can protect us from our brutal inner desires.

☑ Explore whether the novel is an anti-religious text

Yet this hope is destroyed with the death of Simon, who is murdered in a frenzy of blood-lust with the boys chanting **'kill the beast! Cut his throat! Spill his blood!'** There is a sacrificial element to Simon's death, again reflecting his association with Christ who was murdered by his own people. Simon's death marks a changing point in the novel as the boys' descent into savagery is now unstoppable; by killing Simon, who embodies spirituality and goodness, they are now free to unleash the darkness within them and any positive power of religion is easily disposed of with the murder of Simon. Indeed, the boys seem to use religion as a means of exploring their inner savagery. An example of this is just before Simon's death when Jack is elevated to god-like status; the hunters drag out a log where **'Jack, painted and garlanded, sat there like an idol'**. With this status of a deity to be worshipped, he is able to whip the boys into violence which ends in murder. Golding is possibly suggesting that humankind needs religion to justify our natural brutality. This inner brutality or evil is linked to ideas of the devil; the boys give tributes such as the pig's head to the beast out of fear and reverence for the power that they think the beast holds. This pagan practice to avert supernatural evil is something the boys quickly turn to and the pig's head on the stick is named the 'Lord of the Flies' which translates into 'Beelzebub' in Greek, which is a name for the devil. Golding did hold religious beliefs but was not a member of an established church and he explores a number of ideas about faith within the novel. It is Simon who realises that the evil is an intrinsic part of human nature as he talks to the Lord of the Flies who says **'I'm part of you. Close, close, close!'** There is a sense of *foreshadowing* in the *repetition* of the word **'close'**; each time, the Lord of the Flies reminds Simon just how fragile the human conscience and how fragile the veneer of civilisation is. Simon has the perception to see that the Beast is inside us all, and to recognise the darkness of man's heart. Golding fought in World War Two and saw even the best of men give in to savagery and brutality. Golding viewed the violence and cruelty in us as the 'terrible disease' of being human; he saw evil as an internal force that is part of us. There is no external devil to be frightened of but we should be frightened of ourselves.

☑ Continue to explore whether the novel is an anti-religious text

It would seem, therefore, that 'Lord of the Flies' presents religion as a weak force for the good but possibly a powerful force for savage behaviour. This is evident in the bullying of Piggy. Piggy is defined by his plump build and Jack takes the first opportunity to mock him about this, telling him to **'shut up, Fatty'**. As laughter surrounds him, Piggy is immediately established as a victim, as someone who is physically weaker and therefore open to abuse. Piggy generates hate and contempt; he is a vent for the boys' instinctive dark urges to hurt and humiliate, and Jack leads the way in constantly bullying him. Golding lived through the 1930s and 1940s and would have been aware of the horrific persecution that the Jewish people experienced in Europe. It is possible, in an *allegorical* novel where Jack represents the dictator Hitler, that Piggy represents the Jewish people. Golding illustrates how people are persecuted because of their religion, and how religion can generate terrible hostility.

☑ Finish with an overview

Religious references, both Christian and pagan, weave their way through the novel. While it is possible to view religion as a force for the good in the figure of the Christ figure Simon, there are many instances where religion is presented as a catalyst for evil. This pessimistic presentation fits in with the general message of the novel, that mankind has an **'essential illness'** , and that religion is not powerful enough to contain our inner savagery.

12 Loss of Innocence
Exploration of a Theme

The boys start the novel as innocent young schoolboys but, by the end, they have committed unspeakable acts and have lost this innocence forever.

'happy, heaving pile'

• Simon, Ralph and Jack playfight on the first day's exploration of the island, ending up in a **'happy, heaving pile'**.

• The **adjectives** reflect how the boys enthusistically bond with one another, caught up in the excitement and novelty of their situation. The **noun 'pile'** suggests a mass of cheerful, indiscriminate humanity, merging into one, the epitome of youthful exuberance.

• Interestingly, the playfighting is the way the boys choose to bond with each other; it **foreshadows** a time when the fighting becomes much more serious.

Context: Golding subverts the genre of children's adventure books such as 'Coral Island' and 'Swallows and Amazons'. In these naive stories, the children live outside the world of grown-ups and enjoy great camaraderie and adventure throughout the novels until they are reunited with the adult world at the end. Yet Golding twists this genre to show the bleak savagery at the heart of us all as the boys on the island violently turn on each other.

'Ralph was fighting to get near, to get a handful of that brown, vulnerable flesh'

• Golding shows us that all characters, even the 'good' ones, have an instinct to commit evil acts. Ralph is attracted to the violence of a playfight. The **repetitive clause 'to get'** reflects his burning desire to hurt Robert. In the heat of the moment, Ralph does not see Robert as a frightened human; the **noun 'flesh'** reflects how Ralph has dehumanised Robert in his craving to inflict pain on him. At this point, Ralph begins to see his own darker side, and thus begin to lose his innocence.

Context: Golding fought in World War Two and saw even the best of men give in to savagery and brutality. Ralph's desire to hurt and kill is part of human nature.

'Kill the beast! Cut his throat! Spill his blood!'	• The boys kill Simon in a frenzy of bloodlust; the chant illustrates how the mob mentality has consumed the boys. • The *monosyllabic* words and the *imperative verbs* create a chilling sense of vicious violence with an intent to hurt. • Simon's death marks a changing point in the novel as with this act, the boys' descent into savagery is now unstoppable; by killing Simon, who embodies goodness, they are now free to unleash the darkness within them.	**Context:** Golding was interested in ideas of power and explored these in other novels; his next novel, 'The Inheritors', tells of a group of brutal homo sapiens (men) who use violence to destroy a Neanderthal tribe. Golding's message is that our inner brutality will destroy naivety and innocence.
'Ralph wept for the end of innocence, the darkness of man's heart, and the fall through the air of the true, wise friend called Piggy' 	• At the end of the novel, Ralph stands on the beach and cries. There is huge *pathos* in Ralph's tears as he sees how he has lost his childhood and witnessed unspeakable acts. Yet his recognition of the **'darkness of man's heart'** gives the reader hope that we can learn from our experiences and so build up a defence against the instincts towards savagery. The noble language of **'true, wise friend'** elevates and honours Piggy; in this, there is hope for the future and that innocence may be lost but barbaric savagery does not have to replace it.	**Context:** In this sense, the novel is a *bildungsroman*, a genre where the central character learns maturity. Ralph has learnt about the dark side of human nature and cannot forget this, returning to civilisation as a changed character.

Grade 9 Exploration:
Exploration of a theme

How does Golding *structure* the novel to illustrate the loss of innocence?

The novel follows the classic story structure of *exposition*, *rising action*, *climax* and *falling action* in a straightforward chronological order which allows the reader to follow each step of the boys' descent into savagery. Yet Golding uses other structural techniques to enable the reader to see the painful journey of the boys from a state of innocence to that of dreadful knowledge.

Flashback
Golding allows us to see the events unfold through the main character of Ralph, and after some time on the island, Ralph has a flashback to a family home in Dartmoor. His memories are full of gentle details such as cornflakes and books which sharply contrast with the harsh wild reality of the island life. This *flashback* allows us to see just how much Ralph has changed from the innocent boy at home with his parents.

Shift in Narrative Voice
Golding also uses a switch in narrative voice to reveal the loss of innocence; we see the events from Simon's point of view as he meets the Lord of the Flies and fully understands that the evil on the island is within themselves as the Lord of the Flies says **'I'm part of you. Close, close, close!'** With its words, Simon realises that the evil is an intrinsic part of human nature. There is a sense of foreshadowing in the *repetition* of the words **'close'**; each time, the Lord of the Flies reminds Simon just how fragile is the human conscience and the veneer of civilisation, and with this understanding, Simon loses his sense of innocence.

Repeated Events
Repeated events are also used by Golding; in the opening chapter, the boys explore the island with cheerful excitement but later they explore the island again, looking for the beast, in a spirit of fear and tension.

Golding possibly uses 'Lord of the Flies' to present a religious *allegory* with the boys beginning the novel in a wonderful Garden of Eden and then falling into sin and darkness. This is reflected in the repeated exploration of the island, showing how everything has changed and how the boys' innocence has been lost.

The *adjectives* reflect the boys' cheerful enthusiasm and naive delight in their situation.

The boys' inner savagery begins to be unleashed. The *repetitive clause* 'to get' reflects Ralph's burning desire to hurt Robert. He begins to lose his innocence.

'happy, heaving pile'

'Ralph was fighting to get near, to get a handful of that brown, vulnerable flesh'

The boys start their adventures in a state of innocence.

The boys soon start to be corrupted.

Loss of Innocence

By the end, the loss of innocence is complete.

How does Golding *structure* the novel to show the loss of innocence?

'Ralph wept for the end of innocence, the darkness of man's heart, and the fall through the air of the true, wise friend called Piggy'

Flashback: Ralph's *flashback* to his home in Dartmoor contrasts with the island's savagery and reflects how much he has changed.

There is huge pathos in Ralph's tears as he sees how he has lost his childhood and witnessed unspeakable acts.

Repeated events: The boys explore the island with cheerful excitement. Later, they explore again but in a spirit of fear and tension.

Sample GCSE Exam Question

How does 'Lord of the Flies' present ideas about the loss of innocence?

Sample GCSE Answer

☑ Start with an overview about the idea of loss of innocence in the novel

In Golding's dystopian novel, 'Lord of the Flies', the boys begin their adventure as innocent young schoolboys but, by the end, they have committed unspeakable acts and have lost this innocence forever. Golding relentlessly takes the reader on a painful journey of this corruption of innocence, exploring the savagery that lies within us all.

☑ Make the point that the boys begin the story in a state of innocence

The novel opens with the stranded boys meeting each other and exploring the island. In their early excitement, Simon, Ralph and Jack playfight during the first day's exploration of the island, ending up in a **'happy, heaving pile'**. The *adjectives* capture how the boys enthusiastically bond with one another, caught up in the excitement and novelty of their situation. The *noun* **'pile'** suggests a mass of cheerful, indiscriminate humanity, merging into one, the epitome of youthful exuberance. Interestingly, the harmless playfighting is the way the boys choose to bond with each other; it *foreshadows* a time when the fighting becomes much more serious. Golding subverts the genre of children's adventure books such as 'Coral Island' and 'Swallows and Amazons'. In these naive stories, the children live outside the world of grown-ups and enjoy great camaraderie and adventure throughout the novels until they are reunited with the adult world at the end. Yet Golding twists this genre to expose the bleak savagery at the heart of us all as the boys on the island violently turn on each other, leaving innocent adventuring behind them as a distant memory.

☑ Move to the point that the boys soon begin to lose their innocence

Certainly, the early simplicity of the island's adventures is soon replaced with darker activities such as hunting. Golding shows us that all characters, even the 'good' ones, have an instinct to commit evil acts. An example of this is when Ralph gets caught up in the taunting of Robert when the boys pretend that he is a pig and use him in a playful hunt which hovers on the edge of real violenc. Ralph is attracted to the violence and **'was fighting to get near, to get a handful of that brown, vulnerable flesh'**. The *repetitive clause* **'to get'** reflects his burning desire to hurt Robert. In the heat of the moment, Ralph does not see Robert as a frightened human; the *noun* **'flesh'** captures how Ralph has dehumanised Robert in his craving to overpower and inflict pain on him. At this point, Ralph begins to give vent to his own darker side, and thus begin to lose his innocence. Golding fought in World War Two and saw even the best of men give in to savagery and brutality. He allows us to see that Ralph's desire to hurt and kill is part of human nature.

As time wears on, this inner desire is allowed full rein and in a very short time the boys have moved from playfighting to murder as the boys kill Simon in a frenzy of blood-lust, shouting **'kill the beast! Cut his throat! Spill his blood!'** The chant illustrates the mob mentality that has consumed the boys. The ***monosyllabic*** words and the ***imperative verbs*** create a chilling sense of vicious violence. Simon's death marks a changing point in the novel as, with this act, the boys' descent into savagery is now unstoppable; by killing Simon, who embodies goodness, they are now free to unleash the darkness and violence within them. Golding was interested in ideas of power and explored these in other novels; his next novel, 'The Inheritors', tells of a group of brutal homo sapiens (men) who use violence to destroy a Neanderthal tribe. Golding's message is that our inner brutality will destroy naivety and innocence. Ralph recognises this by the end of the novel as he **'wept for the end of innocence, the darkness of man's heart, and the fall through the air of the true, wise friend called Piggy'**. There is huge ***pathos*** in Ralph's tears as he sees how he has lost his childhood and witnessed unspeakable acts yet his recognition of the **'darkness of man's heart'** gives the reader hope that we can learn from our experiences and so build up a defence against the instincts towards savagery. The noble language of **'true, wise friend'** elevates and honours Piggy; in this, there is hope for the future and that innocence may be lost but barbaric savagery does not have to replace it. In this sense, the novel is a ***bildungsroman***, a genre where the central character learns maturity. Ralph has learnt about the dark side of human nature and cannot forget this, returning to civilisation as a changed character.

☑ Explore how Golding uses structural techniques to reflect the boys' corruption

The novel follows the classic story structure of ***exposition, rising action, climax*** and ***falling action*** in a straightforward chronological order which allows the reader to follow each step of the boys' descent into savagery. Yet Golding uses other structural techniques to enable the reader to follow the painful journey of the boys from a state of innocence to that of dreadful knowledge. Golding allows us to see most of the events unfold through the main character of Ralph, and after some time on the island, Ralph has a ***flashback*** to a family home in Dartmoor. His memories are full of gentle details such as cornflakes and books which sharply contrast with the harsh wild reality of the island life. This ***flashback*** allows us to see just how much Ralph has changed from the innocent boy at home with his parents. Golding also uses a switch in ***narrative voice*** to reveal the loss of innocence; we see the events from Simon's point of view as he meets the Lord of the Flies and fully understands that the evil on the island is within themselves: the Lord of the Flies says **'I'm part of you. Close, close, close!'** With its words, Simon who realises that the evil is an intrinsic part of human nature. There is a sense of ***foreshadowing*** in the ***repetition*** of the words **'close'**; each time, the Lord of the Flies reminds Simon just how fragile is the human conscience and the veneer of civilisation, and, with this understanding, Simon loses his sense of innocence. ***Repeated*** events are another device used by Golding; in the opening chapter, the boys explore the island with cheerful excitement but later they explore the island again, looking for the beast, in a spirit of fear and tension. Golding possibly uses 'Lord of the Flies' to present a religious ***allegory*** with the boys beginning the novel in a wonderful Garden of Eden and then falling into sin and darkness. This is reflected in the ***repeated*** exploration of the island, showing how everything has changed and how the boys' innocence has been lost.

☑ Finish with an overview

'Lord of the Flies' presents us with a story of a group of boys who begin their adventures in a state of cheerful innocence but are corrupted by their own inner natures. Human nature causes their state of innocence to crumble until the boys are savages, ruled entirely by primitive urges and the fear of violence. Golding leaves us with a pessimistic view of how the loss of innocence is both inevitable and incredibly painful.

Quotations
Recap & Revise

Chapter One: The Sound of the Shell

'vision of red and yellow... witch-like cry'

A bird makes a sound which is a **'witch-like cry'**.

'mildness... that proclaimed no devil'

Ralph is a character who has an innate goodness.

'We can use this to call the others'

Piggy understands how the conch can be used to summon the separated boys into one place.

'flung themselves down and lay grinning and panting at Ralph like dogs'

The cheerful twins are compared to dogs.

'something dark was fumbling along'

The boys watch the choir move along the beach.

'eyes, frustrated now, turning, or ready to turn, to anger'

Jack's eyes show his short temper when he first meets Ralph.

'kept to himself with an inner intensity of avoidance and secrecy'

Roger is a quiet, withdrawn boy.

'smiled pallidly'

Simon is physically different to the other boys as he faints and 'smiled pallidly'.

'Piggy' 'Shut up, Fatty' 'Laughter arose...'

Piggy is defined by his plump build and Jack takes the first opportunity to mock him about this.

'his size, and attractive appearance'

Ralph is tall and good-looking.

'him with the shell'

Ralph is linked to the conch and elected as leader of the boys.

'Better Piggy than Fatty," he said at last, with the directness of true leadership'

Ralph betrays his new friend Piggy by telling the boys of the nickname that Piggy is ashamed of.

'The creepers were as thick as their thighs... This is real exploring'

Ralph, Simon and Jack excitedly investigate the island on their first day, finding thick creepers that need to crawled through.

'happy, heaving pile'

The boys playfight as they explore the island.

Chapter Two: Fire on the Mountain

'like a crowd of kids'

Piggy despairs of the way the boys rush off with no order or plans.

'strange invisible light of friendship, adventure and content'

Jack and Ralph sit in front of the fire they have jointly made, pleased with their work and enjoying each other's company.

'We're not savages. We're English and the English are the best at everything'

Jack agrees with Ralph that there should be rules on the island.

'Piggy was an outsider, not only by accent, which did not matter, but by fat'

It is his physical shape which immediately marks him as a victim, not his social class.

Chapter Three: Huts on the Beach

'we want meat' 'we need shelters'

Jack and Ralph's friendship is tested by their different priorities.

'pulled off the choicest' (fruit)

Simon takes fruit from the trees to give to the littleuns;

'candle-like buds'

Simon withdraws into the forest to be alone with nature.

Chapter Four: Painted Faces and Long Hair

'Roger's arm was conditioned by a civilisation that knew nothing of him and was in ruins'

Roger throws stones at the littleuns but holds back from hurting them with a direct aim.

'The mask was a thing of its own, behind which Jack hid, liberated from shame and self-consciousness'

Jack paints his face in coloured mud, creating a mask.

'link... snapped and fastened elsewhere'

After the confrontation over the dead fire and the failed attempt to be rescued, Jack and Ralph's friendship changes.

Chapter Five: Beast from Water

'mankind's essential illness'

Simon undertands how we all have the capacity for violence.

'Life,' said Piggy expansively, 'is scientific, that's what it is. In a year or two when the war's over they'll be travelling to Mars and back'

Piggy firmly believes in the power of science and rational thought.

'the rules are the only thing we've got!'

'bollocks to the rules! We're strong- we hunt!'

Ralph is aware of the importance of rules as the foundation of their society but Jack dismisses these rules.

Chapter Six: Beast from the Air

'Boy -you- are- driving -me- slowly -insane!'

Sam and Eric mimic their irate schoolteacher while they are on fire duty, giggling as they recall his shouts.

'Couldn't let you do it on your own'

Jack follows Ralph into Castle Rock.

'rotten place' 'wizard fort'

When they find Castle Rock, Ralph calls it a **'rotten place'** while Jack sees it as a **'wizard fort'**.

Chapter Seven: Shadows and Tall Trees

'We'll go and look'

Ralph announces his intention of climbing the mountain to see if there is a beast.

'Ralph was fighting to get near, to get a handful of that brown, vulnerable flesh'
Ralph gets caught up in the taunting of Robert when the boys pretend that he is a pig and use him in a playful hunt which hovers on the edge of real violence.

Chapter Eight: A Gift for the Darkness

'I'm part of you. Close, close, close!'
It is Simon who realises that the evil is an intrinsic part of human nature as he talks to the Lord of the Flies.

Chapter Nine: A View to a Death

'Jack, painted and garlanded, sat there like an idol'
Jack is elevated to god-like status

'The dark sky was shattered by a blue white scar'
Simon is killed in the middle of a storm.

'Kill the beast! Cut his throat! Spill his blood!'
The boys kill Simon in a frenzy of blood-lust.

Chapter Ten: The Shell and the Glasses

'I was on the outside too'
The boys lie to each other about their involvement in Simon's death.

'The chief was sitting there, naked to the waist... he pointed at this savage and that with his spear'
Towards the end, Jack is in total control of his hunters.

'We gave them something to think about' ... **'At least you did. I got myself mixed up with myself in a corner.'**

Sam displays a rueful honesty when the hunters steal Piggy's glasses; dissecting the fight, Sam's brave claim that **'We gave them something to think about'** is soon changed to **'At least you did. I got myself mixed up with myself in a corner.'**

Chapter Eleven: Castle Rock

'Because what's right right. Give me my glasses'
Piggy practises what he will say to Jack in order to get his stolen glasses back.

'Samneric protested out of the heart of civilization. "Oh, I say!" "—honestly!"'
Sam and Eric are taken captive by Jack's tribe.

'exploded into a thousand white fragments'
Piggy is killed as he holds the conch which completely smashes during the fall.

'only just avoiding pushing him with his shoulder'
Roger takes over the torture of Sam and Eric, pushing past Jack and **'only just avoiding pushing him with his shoulder'.**

Chapter Twelve: The Cry of the Hunters

'screaming,snarling, bloody'
Ralph fights for his life at the end.

'white drill, epaulettes, a revolver'
Ralph is saved by a naval officer who is equipped with **'white drill, epaulettes, a revolver'.**

'Ralph wept for the end of innocence, the darkness of man's heart, and the fall through the air of the true, wise friend called Piggy'
Ralph cries as he reflects on his time on the island.

Glossary
Explanation of terms

ADJECTIVE - a word that describes a noun **e.g. 'true, wise friend'**

ADVERB - a word that describes a verb **e.g. 'smiled pallidly'**

ALLEGORY - a story that can be interpreted to have a hidden meaning or message

ANTAGONIST - a character who causes conflict for the protagonist

BILDUNGSROMAN - a genre where the central character learns maturity

CHRONOLOGICAL STRUCTURE - when a novel is structured in time order

CLAUSE - a group of words that contains a verb

CLIMAX - the most intense moment of a drama or a story

DECLARATIVE SENTENCE - a sentence that states a fact **e.g. 'We'll go and look'**

DIALOGUE - conversation between characters

EXCLAMATORY PHRASE OR SENTENCE - a sentence or phrase that shows excitement or emotion **e.g. 'the rules are the only thing we've got!'**

EXPOSITION - the background information to a character in a story

FORESHADOWING - to give a warning of a future event **e.g. the description of Jack's choir as 'something dark was fumbling along' foreshadows the savagery the boys will descend to.**

IMAGE - powerful words or phrase that paints a picture in our heads

IMPERATIVE VERBS - verbs that give orders e.g. '**Kill** the beast!'

INTENSIFIER - word that strengthens an adverb or adjective **e.g. 'so persuasively'**

JUXTAPOSITION - see contrast

LIST - a group of ordered items or actions **e.g. 'screaming,snarling, bloody'**

METAPHOR - desciribing a person or object as something else **e.g. 'link... snapped and fastened elsewhere'**

MODAL VERBS - verbs that show a level of certainty **e.g. 'We'll go and look'**

MONOSYLLABIC WORDS -words with one syllable **e.g. 'Kill the beast!'**

MOTIF - a recurring idea that helps explore a theme

NOUN - name of an object/place/time/emotion

PATHOS - sadness

PLOT DEVICE - technique used to move narrative along

PROTAGONIST - the leading character in a novel

REPETITION - when a word or phrase is repeated e.g. '**close, close, close!'**

RISING ACTION - events that build up drama/tension/plot

SETTING- where a scene is played out **e.g. the story's setting is on the island**

SIMILE - describing a person or object as something else using 'like' or 'as' **e.g. 'witch-like cry'**

STRUCTURE - the order in which events happen in a story

SUPERLATIVE ADJECTIVE - the most extreme comparative adjective **e.g. 'the choicest fruit'**

SYMBOL - when an object/person stands for something else **e.g the conch is used as a symbol of democracy**

SYNTAX - order of words in a sentence

TONE- mood or atmosphere